WASHITA

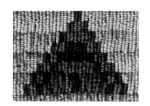

WASHITA

By Mary Jane Warde

National Park Service for Washita Battlefield National Historic Site

Oklahoma Historical Society

2003

Published by the Oklahoma Historical Society, Oklahoma City, Oklahoma, and the National Park Service for Washita Battlefield National Historic Site, Cheyenne, Oklahoma, through Cooperative Agreement 1443CA125098002, Modifications 1-6.

September 1, 2003

TABLE OF CONTENTS

LIST OF ILLUSTRATIONS

Maps

Figures

PREFACE

This book is the comprehensive report on a five-phase project conducted by the Oklahoma Historical Society under contract with the National Park Service. Between 1999 and 2003, staff from the Oklahoma Historical Society and Dr. Loretta Fowler, an anthropologist and private contractor, conducted research on the human occupation of the Washita Battlefield National Historic Site and the association of various peoples with the land over time. Tribes found to be associated with the site and that cooperated during this project include the Cheyenne and Arapaho Tribes, Apache Tribes of Oklahoma, Caddo Tribe, Chickasaw Nation, Choctaw Nation, Comanche Nation, Kiowa Tribe, and Wichita and Affiliated Tribes. The purpose of the project was to collect information that would be used in the development of the site. The researchers also hoped to learn through a series of interviews what the communities in the area, including the Indian communities, think about the site and what meaning it holds for them.

The purpose for the creation of Washita Battlefield National Historic Site was, of course, to commemorate the Washita Massacre—the attack of the Seventh Cavalry, led by Lt. Col. George Armstrong Custer, on the camp of Cheyenne Peace Chief Black Kettle on November 27, 1868. That event, tied closely to the Sand Creek Massacre of 1864 and the Battle of the Little Bighorn in 1876, created a wound that has still not healed after more than a century. However, the researchers found that the Washita River Valley in western Oklahoma has been important to many peoples over the centuries. The experience of each of those diverse groups and cultures provides context for the development of the site and understanding of the event it commemorates.

ACKNOWLEDGMENTS

Phase V of the Washita Project, the comprehensive report prepared by the Oklahoma Historical Society (OHS) for Washita Battlefield National Historic Site (WBNHS) and the National Park Service (NPS), resulted from the contributions of many individuals: private citizens and NPS staff, Indian and non-Indian people; and scholarly, tribal, and amateur historians dedicated to preserving the local, state, and tribal past. Special thanks are due to Dr. Alexa Roberts, NPS, and to Sarah Craighead, Superintendent at WBNHS during four of the five years of this project. They were a pleasure to work with.

Phase I, which dealt with Cheyenne and other tribal memories of the Washita Massacre, owed much to Rodger Harris, Oral Historian, OHS, and to field workers Jim Anquoe (Kiowa) and Larry Roman Nose (Cheyenne). In Phases II and III, Dr. Loretta Fowler conducted fine ethnographic studies of Cheyenne and other tribes' association with the event and the vicinity of the Washita Massacre, respectively, with the aid of field workers Jim Anquoe and Moses Starr (Cheyenne). This comprehensive report would not be possible without her and their contributions. Rodger Harris and Dennis W. Zotigh (Kiowa/Pueblo/Lakota), Tribal Research and Relations Specialist, OHS, contributed to Phase IV, the ethnographic study of non-Indian association with the former Cheyenne and Arapaho Reservation, focusing on the WBNHS vicinity. Volunteer Bob Bish, OHS, assisted with additional research and duplication. Judith Michener, Assistant Oral Historian, OHS, produced the audio- and videotapes. Vicky Gardner transcribed most of the interviews performed as a result of this five-phase project. Chester Cowen (Choctaw) and Lillie Kerr (Seminole/Choctaw) of the OHS Photographic Archives contributed time and expertise in selecting and scanning images. Bill Siemens, Graphic Artist, OHS, adapted historic maps from the OHS archival collections. Mary Ann Blochowiak, Editor, *The Chronicles of Oklahoma*, OHS, prepared the manuscript for publication.

Also, many thanks are due to the tribal officials and cultural officers who reviewed drafts and recommended knowledgeable people for interviews. They were from the following:

- Cheyenne and Arapaho Tribes
- Apache Tribe of Oklahoma
- Caddo Tribe
- Chickasaw Nation
- Choctaw Nation
- Comanche Nation
- Kiowa Tribe
- Wichita and Affiliated Tribes

Lastly, thanks are due to the interviewees, both Indian and non-Indian, who welcomed us into their homes, gave us their time, and provided the information and perspectives needed to complete this project.

To all of them, thank you and *aho*!

Dr. Mary Jane Warde
Indian Historian
Oklahoma Historical Society

INTRODUCTION

In order to gather information needed for the development of Washita Battlefield National Historic Site near Cheyenne, Oklahoma and to contribute to the historical record, staff members from the Oklahoma Historical Society and Dr. Loretta Fowler, an anthropologist and private contractor, conducted a five-phase project at the request of the National Park Service. The researchers used standard investigative techniques of the disciplines of history and anthropology. This included studying, among other things, documents, maps, federal and state records, Indian records, newspapers, and photographs. It also included the collection of oral history, both of Indian and non-Indian communities associated with the site. The phases of the project were as follows:

    I.   Collection of Cheyenne oral history about the Washita Massacre

    II. Collection of Cheyenne oral traditions about their association with the site of Washita Battlefield National Historic Site

    III. Collection of oral traditions about the association of other Indian peoples with the vicinity of Washita Battlefield National Historic Site

    IV. Collection of documentation and interviews of non-Indians about their association with the vicinity of Washita Battlefield National Historic Site

    V. Compilation and creation of this comprehensive report

The researchers worked closely with communities historically associated with the location of Washita Battlefield National Historic Site. This included contacting several Indian tribes: the Cheyenne and Arapaho Tribes, Wichita and Affiliated Tribes, Caddo Tribe, Kiowa Tribe, Comanche Nation, Apache Tribe of Oklahoma, Choctaw Nation, and Chickasaw Nation. Each appointed a knowledgeable representative to work with the researchers or to provide the requested information. This project could not have succeeded without their cooperation. The researchers also contacted non-Indians associated with towns and communities in the former Cheyenne and Arapaho Reservation. The geographic area covered in the project thus included all or part of Ellis, Dewey, Blaine, Kingfisher, Custer, Canadian, Beckham, and Washita counties in western Oklahoma, as well as Roger Mills County, the site of Washita Battlefield National Historic Site (See Map 1).

The researchers discovered that human occupation of the vicinity of Washita Battlefield National Historic Site by peoples known today goes back to about 800 A.D. Historical documentation collected during this project spans the last four centuries. In addition, the researchers collected interviews of fifty-nine people, Indian and non-Indian, whose association with the area around Washita Battlefield National Historic Site spanned the period from 1908 to 2003. First-person memories and experiences addressed the meaning of the site as well as a wide range of topics: the varied Indian cultures, the uses of resources in the Washita River Valley, Indian life in the twentieth century, non-Indian settlement of the Washita River Valley, the impact of the Dust Bowl and the Great Depression, the reclamation of the land through conservation in the second half of the twentieth century, and the rich literary and artistic tradition, somewhat surprising in sparsely populated western Oklahoma, that reflects the history and cultures of the area.

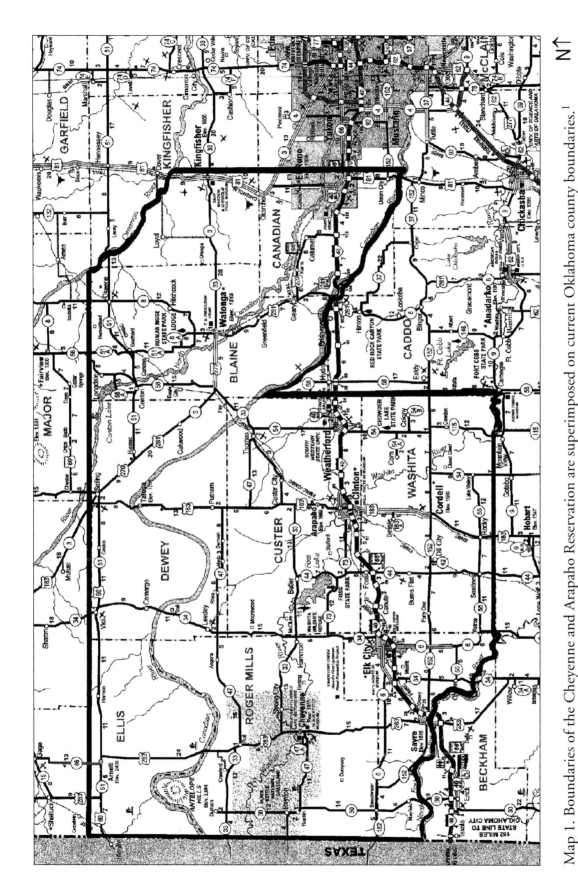

Map 1. Boundaries of the Cheyenne and Arapaho Reservation are superimposed on current Oklahoma county boundaries.[1]

[1] Detail of "2001–2002 Official State Map," Oklahoma Department of Transportation, Oklahoma City, Oklahoma.

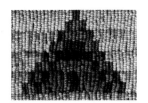

ONE MORNING AT DAYBREAK

Near midnight on November 26, 1868, Lt. Col. George Armstrong Custer and two Osage trailers followed a pony trail, clearly visible under a full moon, through foot-deep snow toward the Washita River. With him were additional scouts; behind him a half-mile back, with orders against loud talking, smoking, or striking matches, were eleven companies of the Seventh Cavalry, seven ammunition wagons, and an ambulance. In the saddle since four that morning, the troopers waited in near-zero temperatures and hard-crusted snow, while their commander went on ahead with the scouts. Custer was elated. In professional disgrace for the last several months, he had only recently returned to active duty to participate in Maj. Gen. Philip Sheridan's campaign against the Plains tribes. Success in the campaign would help redeem the reputation and career of the "Boy General" of the Civil War. In heavy snow on November 23, they had left Camp Supply at the junction of Wolf and Beaver Creeks, heading generally toward where they believed they would find the Cheyenne and Arapaho winter camps. At noon three days later, while the expedition halted on the icy Canadian River near the Antelope Hills, scout Jack Corbin came in with word that Maj. Joel Elliott, scouting upstream, had come across fresh pony tracks leading south. Custer left his supply train and caught up with Elliott. As Custer and the scouts looked down from a ridge north of the Washita River, the scent of a fire, barking dogs, a tinkling horse bell, and a baby's cry convinced them there was indeed an Indian camp in the timber on the other bank.[1]

Although Hard Rope, Little Beaver, and the other Osage trailers were concerned about attacking a camp without good information on its identity or size, Custer quickly called his officers together and planned a dawn attack that would split his troops into four columns. Elliott was to circle around the camp and strike from the northeast. Capt. William Thompson would attack from the southwest. Two columns, including Custer, the Osages, the sharpshooters, and the regimental band, would attack frontally. Each column was to get as close to the camp as possible, which meant covering several miles as silently as possible in the frigid darkness (See Map 2).[2]

[1] W. S. Nye, *Carbine and Lance: The Story of Old Fort Sill* (Norman: University of Oklahoma Press, 1937, 1969 edition), 60–63; "Custer's Washita Fight," *New York Sun*, May 14, 1899, Fred S. Barde Collection, Oklahoma Historical Society, Oklahoma City, Oklahoma.

[2] Nye, *Carbine and Lance*, 62–63.

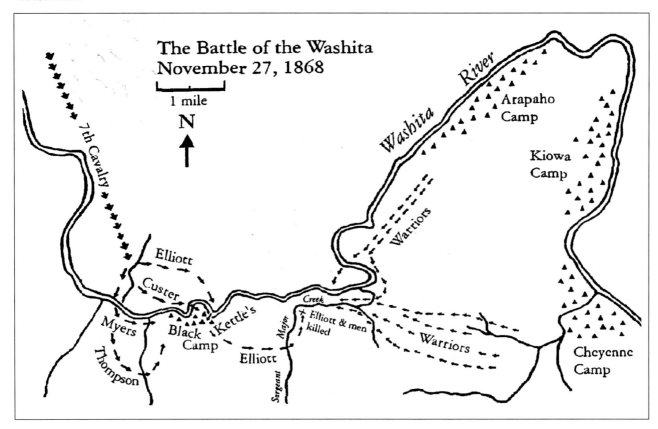

Map 2. Washita Battlefield on November 27, 1868[3]

In 1904 Ben Clark, Custer's chief of scouts, returned to the site and recalled:

> Custer quickly formed his plan of battle. Captain Myers was sent to the right, and told to occupy the high ground south of the village, to cut off retreat. He moved cautiously, forded the river close to where a little stream empties in from the south and passed up this little tributary several hundred yards to the higher land. [Capt. Louis McLane] Hamilton and [Col. Albert] Barnitz went with their detachments to the heavy timber down the river northeast of the village. [Col. W. W.] Cook's sharpshooters took a stand on the north side of the Washita. . . . About half a mile north and west of the village, Custer formed his five troops in line of battle. Close by was his regimental band which was to signal the attack by playing "Garry Owen."[4]

The sleeping camp was Cheyenne and sheltered the followers of Black Kettle, who had survived a dawn attack almost exactly four years earlier at Sand Creek, Colorado Territory. As a peace chief, Black Kettle worked to avoid conflict. Knowing that a fresh effort was under way to force the Cheyennes onto the reservation established one year earlier, he had just returned from a visit to Col. W. B. Hazen at Fort Cobb farther down the Washita River. Hazen, al-

[3] *Washita Battlefield National Historic Site Bulletin*, Washita Battlefield National Historic Site, Cheyenne, Oklahoma.

[4] "Custer's Oklahoma Fight," unidentified newspaper clipping, 1904, "Battle of the Washita," Section X, Oklahoma Historical Society, Oklahoma City, Oklahoma. The scout spelled his name both "Clark" and "Clarke."

though sympathetic, had told Black Kettle to make his peace with Gen. Philip Sheridan. When Black Kettle returned to his camp, he found that some of his people were anxious, while others were complacent. In the winter Indians and troops alike generally kept to the shelter of their camps and barracks. Two days before, some Kiowas, returning from a raid against the Utes, had come across a trail of shod horses. They reported it to the Cheyennes, but were ignored.[5]

Another Kiowa, Eonahpah, according to his great-granddaughter, reported the same sighting. He had been hunting for the past few days and had fixed a small shelter up on the hillside to be out of the snow. He came down to Black Kettle's camp that night, ate with the Cheyennes, and declined their invitation to stay and celebrate their return from a recent raid. Instead, he went back to his shelter, took off his moccasins, and lay down to sleep. His hosts paid his story no heed. While he slept, they danced late into the night.[6]

Others, however, wanted to avoid any danger. Moving Behind, then a fourteen-year-old orphan, lived with an aunt and her husband Roll Down. Moving Behind recalled, "I felt rather strange late that evening. . . ." Black Kettle's wife, Medicine Woman Later, had been seriously wounded at Sand Creek but had survived. Moving Behind recalled that she "became very angry, and stood outside for a long time because they were unable to move that evening. She was disappointed. Sometimes your feelings tell you things ahead; perhaps this was what that woman felt. She talked excitedly, and said, 'I don't like this delay, we could have moved long ago. The Agent sent word for us to leave at once. It seems we are crazy and deaf, and cannot hear.'"[7]

The Cheyennes sleeping in the lodges beside the river heard nothing as the soldiers moved in near dawn. Finally even the one man on guard went into his lodge to get out of the cold. The cavalrymen were already close when the Cheyennes realized their danger. A single shot alerted the camp, then a few notes of "Garry Owen" sounded before the intense cold silenced the bugle. Moving Behind remembered, "We heard a woman saying in a low voice: 'Wake up! Wake up! White men are here!'"[8] People half-dressed scrambled out of the lodges and into the cold dawn. Moving Behind heard her aunt call and ran out of the lodge. "I could see the dark figures of persons running here and there in a mad rush," Moving Behind remembered. "When a burst of gunfire was heard, my aunt would catch my hand, and say, 'hold my hand tightly, don't turn it loose whatever may happen. We will go somewhere and hide.'"[9]

Custer wrote in his field report on the assault that when the signal came three of the four columns charged as one, and the other was just slightly late. Custer stated, "There never was a more complete surprise. My men charged the village and reached the lodges before

5 William H. Leckie, *The Military Conquest of the Southern Plains* (Norman: University of Oklahoma Press, 1963), 92–101.

6 Interview of Martha Koomsa (Perez), by Mary Jane Warde and Jim Anquoe, Carnegie, Oklahoma, July 14, 1999, in Mary Jane Warde, *Final Report on Cooperative Agreement No. 1443CA125098002, Modification 1, Conduct Oral History Research for Washita Historical Site* (hereafter cited as *Final Report, Phase I*), National Park Service, September 30, 1999.

7 Quoted in Theodore A. Ediger and Vinnie Hoffman, "Some Reminiscences of the Battle of the Washita," *The Chronicles of Oklahoma* 33 (Summer 1955):137–138.

8 Quoted in Ediger and Hoffman, "Reminiscences," 138.

9 Ibid., 138–139.

Figure 1. Lt. Col. George Armstrong Custer commanded the Seventh Cavalry attack on Chief Black Kettle's village on the Washita River. *Oklahoma Historical Society*

the Indians were aware of our presence. The moment the charge was ordered the band struck up "Garry Owen," and with cheers that strongly reminded me of scenes during the [Civil] war, every trooper, led by his officer, rushed towards the village."[10]

Clark recalled, "The horses sprang forward on a run, the troopers shouting in anticipation of battle. The musicians had little time for music. Their horses became uncontrollable in the rush and rumble of the charge, and a number of the musicians were drawn into the very teeth of the fight."[11]

Custer, mounted on a black stallion, and Clark jumped the narrow Washita River where the trail crossed it and charged through the camp. After shooting a Cheyenne man in his path, Custer took a position on a little knoll that offered a good view of the fighting. He issued orders from there. Custer provided few details of the fight in his field report, but merely said, "The lodges and all their contents were in our possession within 10 minutes after the charge was ordered, but the real fighting, such as has rarely if ever been equaled in Indian warfare, began when attempting to clear out or kill the warriors posted in ravines and underbrush; charge after charge was made, and most gallantly, too, but the Indians had resolved to sell their lives as dearly as possible."[12]

Amithneh, a Cheyenne girl who was eight or nine at the time, told her great-granddaughter about that dawn. When the shooting

[10] Report of Lieutenant Colonel G. A. Custer to Major General P. H. Sheridan, in the field on Washita River, November 28, 1868, 40th Cong., 3d sess., S. Ex. Doc. 18, 27.

[11] "Custer's Oklahoma Fight."

[12] Custer to Sheridan, November 28, 1868, 28.

Figure 2. The only known photograph of Black Kettle (seated first row behind man wearing hat) was taken in 1864 at Camp Weld near Denver. *Western History Collections, University of Oklahoma Libraries.*

started, she, her sister aged five or six, her toddler brother, and her mother Mosaio were asleep in their lodge. Amithneh's father, Black Kettle, stuck his head in the door and told her mother to get the children up and ready to run. Mosaio put her son on her back while Amithneh put on her moccasins and grabbed the little backpack most children had for emergencies. She told her great-granddaughter, "We took out, started running with the rest of the women." The scene was chaotic, and it was impossible to hear. Amithneh said, according to her great-granddaughter:

> . . . The women and children were screaming and crying and the shooting and the soldiers on horseback were just riding every which way. And the men were shouting to each other, and everybody was running. And we followed our mother. I was holding my sister by the hand, but just before we got to the banks of the river, I heard my mother call my name. . . As I turned around, I saw my little brother just tumbling head over heals . . . It knocked the wind out of him, and my little sister ran to pick him up. . . . I ran to my mother and tried to raise her up.

Figure 3. Cheyenne girl about the age of Amithneh. *Oklahoma Historical Society*

> I just lifted one arm, and I could see her eyes were already glassy. And she said take care of your brother and sister. Run down with the rest of the women. And she said, "Don't look back."

Amithneh started to cry.

> My mother told me, "Don't cry. Go! Go and do what I tell you. . . . " I had to leave her and take my little brother by the hand. . . . He couldn't run so we had him by one hand each and he was just dangling between the two of us. . . . We ran down to the bank . . . I looked back to my mother and she had her face on the ground. . . . I knew she was dead. She was shot in the back. . . . I don't know how they missed the baby, but I guess that he was situated in such a way that it went—the shot must have gone between his legs.

The children ran with others fleeing toward the river, trying to take shelter under its banks. Around them, the scene was horrific. Amithneh stated, "I saw two soldiers on horseback. They were chasing a pregnant woman, and they shot her. As she fell, one of them jumped off his horse and sliced her stomach and he held up that unborn baby on his saber. And they were laughing."

Those who could were running down the river toward the safety of other Indian camps. Amithneh and her sister ran with them. She continued, "You could hear the thin sheet of ice cracking as people were jumping in. . . ." Wading in water up to her thighs, she carried her little brother.[13]

[13] Interview of Colleen Cometsevah, by Mary Jane Warde, Clinton, Oklahoma, August 20, 1999, in Warde, *Final Report, Phase I.*

Ben Clark watched as the Cheyennes fleeing down the river fell under the fire of the sharpshooters or ran into Elliott's and Thompson's columns. "...It was here the greatest slaughter took place," he said. "Squaws with their children climbed the steep embankment south of the village and gained the prairie, where Meyers's command lay in wait for them. The Osage scouts, before they could be intercepted, shot down the women and mutilated their bodies. . . ."[14]

Moving Behind and her aunt were among the running Cheyennes. She recalled:

> The air was full of smoke from gunfire, and it was almost impossible to flee, because bullets were flying everywhere. However, somehow we ran and kept running to find a hiding place. As we ran, we could see the red fire of the shots. We got near a hill, and there we saw a steep path, where an old road used to be. There was red grass along the path, and although the ponies had eaten some of it, it was still high enough for us to hide. In this grass we lay flat, our hearts beating fast; and we were afraid to move. It was now bright daylight. It frightened us to listen to the noise and the cries of the wounded. When the noise seemed to quiet down, and we believed the battle was about to end, we raised our heads high enough to see what was going on. We saw a dark figure lying near a hill, and later we learned it was the body of a woman with child. The woman's body had been cut open by the soldiers. The wounded ponies passed near our hiding place, and would moan loudly, just like human beings.[15]

At the first alarm, Black Kettle and his wife, Medicine Woman Later, tried to escape on horseback riding double. Interviewed in 1999, Alfrich Heap of Birds explained how a man told his grandmother, then seven or eight years old, and her older and younger sisters to run down the creek. "As they did they went by Black Kettle, who had been shot, and his wife, and the horse was laying partially on them," Heap of Birds related. "They went on by and they had to jump in the creek to keep from getting shot. This man told them to run down to the village east of there where there is a big, big camp of Cheyennes, Kiowas and Comanches, and to the north, just south of [today's] Strong City, was a village of Arapahos under Little Raven."[16]

In his shelter up on the hillside, Eonapah woke to the commotion, gunfire, and screaming in the Cheyenne camps and rushed outside. His great-granddaughter described what happened then as she heard it from his son, her grandfather:

> . . . And he jumps up and he grabs his bow and arrow and . . . he starts running downhill. As he's running, he couldn't see so much because it was early morning, the haze was so bad, and he said the women and children were just running and screaming,

[14] "Custer's Washita Fight."

[15] Ediger and Hoffman, *Reminiscences*, 139.

[16] Interview of Alfrich Heap of Birds, by Mary Jane Warde and Jim Anquoe, Thomas, Oklahoma, vicinity, July 23, 1999, in Warde, *Final Report, Phase I*.

Figure 4. Eonahpah (Trailing the Enemy), a Kiowa, defended the camp. *Oklahoma Historical Society*

running toward him, and the cavalry men were chasing them and running them down with horses. Then as he was shooting at them, he finally ran out of arrows, and this little boy came running beside him and began handing him his arrows. He must have killed one of the officers, because all of a sudden from behind they just knocked him down and drug him . . . and then they just let him go. He fell in the snow, and as he fell he went hands forward or someway, and his hand caught something and he brought it up, and it was a revolver. I don't think he knew how to shoot it, he just started aiming it, you know. It stunned him, and set them back . . . he was able to save over seventeen women and children. . . . But in all that, the chaos of running out and getting into that skirmish . . . he didn't realize he didn't have his moccasins on—he was barefoot.[17]

Amithneh witnessed the unequal fight. She recalled, "I looked up. There were three men up on the bank. They were shooting and fighting to keep the soldiers away from the people." Two were Cheyenne, but one was the Kiowa. One was shot and fell, but another ran back and picked up a pistol. Amithneh said, "I seen that he had just bow and arrow. . . . They were fighting—those two men were fighting the soldiers as best they could."[18]

The grandmother of Alfrich Heap of Birds also saw them fend off the attacking troopers. She told him, he said, "That Kiowa man, Little Chief, and a man by the name of Packer followed these little

[17] Interview of Martha Koomsa (Perez), by Loretta Fowler and Jim Anquoe, Carnegie, Oklahoma, November 25, 2002, in Loretta Fowler, *Ethnographic Overview (Phase III) for Washita Battlefield National Historical Site*, Cooperative Agreement No. 1443CA125098002 (Modification 4) (hereafter cited as *Final Report, Phase III*, 70.

[18] Interview of Colleen Cometsevah, by Mary Jane Warde, August 20, 1999, in Warde, *Final Report, Phase I*.

Figure 5. Ben Clark served as Custer's chief of scouts. *Oklahoma Historical Society*

girls, and as they came up on a bank . . . these troops were in pursuit. The three of them held off these troops. Mind you, just three of them held off to keep 'em from getting to these little girls. . . . They always said this was the bravest Kiowa they had ever seen that helped these girls to escape. . . ."[19]

Ben Clark, watching from the knoll with Custer, described the scene as he saw it:

> In making its sharp bend around the village, the Washita had cut into its north bank till heavy portions of the bank fell away and made a natural breastwork in the river below. About twenty men, women, and children took refuge in this place and hid from sight during the heaviest fighting. When a lull came they were discovered. They refused to surrender and all were killed.[20]

Custer reported, "One white woman who was in their possession was murdered by her captors the moment we attacked. A white boy held captive, about 10 years old, when about to be rescued, was brutally murdered by a squaw, who ripped out his entrails with a knife."[21] Clark, however, said,

> I saw a Cheyenne woman, the last survivor, kill her child with a butcher knife, and then bury the blade in her own breast. Cheyenne babies are almost as fair as white children. Several of the soldiers thought she had murdered a white child, and one of

19 Interview of Alfrich Heap of Birds, by Mary Jane Warde and Jim Anquoe, Thomas, Oklahoma, vicinity, July 23, 1999, in Warde, *Final Report, Phase I.*

20 "Custer's Oklahoma Fight."

21 Custer to Sheridan, November 28, 1868, 28. The woman was Mrs. Clara Blinn.

them poked his carbine over the embankment and sent a bullet into her brain. In relating this incident in his history of the battle, Custer made the mistake of saying that this woman killed a captive white child.[22]

Custer justified the killing of women and children in his field report: "In the excitement of the fight, as well as in self-defense, it so happened that some of the squaws and a few of the children were killed and wounded. . . . Many of the squaws were taken with arms in their hands, and several of my command are known to have been wounded by them."[23]

According to Clark, he intervened with Custer to stop the killing: "While standing on the knoll to which Custer had ridden, I saw a large number of women and children near two buttes on the prairie south of the village, pursued by Myers's men, who were killing them without mercy. I asked Custer if it was his wish that they should be killed, and he ordered me to stop the slaughter, which I did, placing the captives in a big tepee under guard."[24] Clark found it difficult to take some of the Cheyennes captive. He told a reporter in 1899, "I came upon a wrinkled, grey-haired old squaw, who stood at bay like an enraged tigress. She had an old cavalry saber raised defiantly for battle. She was with difficulty persuaded to lay down the saber after having been assured that her life would be spared." Even after the collection of captives began, Clark said, "The hunting and slaughter of fugitives continued during the greater part of the morning. The Indians fought desperately, but were wholly at a disadvantage. . . . The dusk of the morning gave cover for escape, or the bloodshed would have been greater."[25]

Moving Behind and her aunt watched, terrified, from their hiding place in the tall grass. She remembered, "The soldiers would pass back and forth near the spot where I lay. As I turned sideways and looked, one soldier saw us, and rode toward where we lay. He stopped his horse, and stared at us. He did not say a word, and we wondered what would happen. But he left, and no one showed up after that. I suppose he pitied us, and left us alone."[26]

By then, the noise of the fight had alerted the camps farther downstream. According to Wolf Belly Woman, who had been invited to spend the night in Black Kettle's camp but declined, there was an Arapaho camp downstream, then another Cheyenne camp, and then a Kiowa camp. In the Cheyenne camp Cut Arm (also called Walks Different) got up and stirred the fire for light as he woke his family—daughters Little Woman Curious Horn and White Buffalo Woman and sons Standing Bird, Bird Chief, and Red Bird. According to the account Little Woman Curious Horn related to her descendants, Cut Arm hustled the girls and their mother outside, and

[22] "Custer's Oklahoma Fight."

[23] Custer to Sheridan, November 28, 1868, 29.

[24] "Custer's Oklahoma Fight." In an interview near the turn of the century, Clark repeated his account but said that Custer reacted to his question as if he considered it officious. Interview of Ben Clarke, Walter Camp Collection, University of Indiana, copy in Section X, Oklahoma Historical Society, Oklahoma City, Oklahoma, 7.

[25] "Custer's Washita Fight."

[26] Ediger and Hoffman, "Reminiscences," 139.

Figure 6. As late at the 1930s, pony bones from the Washita Massacre could still be found on the battle site. *Oklahoma Historical Society*

they mounted their best horses, usually kept near the tepee. Then, according to her account,

> . . . He took out his whip and just whipped those horses and told them to keep going and don't come back. . . . Go down to the other camp. And then he and his three sons got on their horses and they went down to help Black Kettle. . . . The youngest one was shot through the stomach, and he fell off his horse and the father Walks Different he jumped off his horse and he gathered up his son in his arms and his son told him, "Keep my horse." And he said, "No, he's going with you." And he kissed him on the cheek and he died right there. And so the father shot that horse, his horse.[27]

Along with other Cheyennes, Kiowas led by Satanta and Arapahos led by Little Raven hurried up the Washita toward the noise of the fight. Along the way, they gave help to at least one fugitive. Magpie, a very young man, was asleep in the lodge next to Black Kettle's when the attack began. He pulled on his clothes and buckled on a pistol just as the first volley struck. With two friends he ran west for the creek only to meet soldiers coming from that direction. They turned south and took cover in a thicket of chinaberries and tall grass, but soldiers shot into the thicket and wounded Magpie just below his left knee. Even so, Magpie ran with his friends, with the sol-

[27] Interview of Colleen Cometsevah, by Mary Jane Warde, August 20, 1999, in Warde, *Final Report, Phase I.*

Figure 7. Little Woman Curious Horn and her daughter in 1897.
Oklahoma Historical Society

diers right behind them. "Just when I thought they would kill us," Magpie said, "they spied a large group of women and children coming from the southeastern end of the village. So they quit chasing us and took after the larger bunch of fugitives." The boys ran past the twin knolls at the top of the hill and down the next valley, going east until they met the men hurrying upstream to help defend the camp. They dressed his leg wound, and left Magpie to go on east toward safety.[28]

Meanwhile, Maj. Joel Elliott, then separated from his command, had been south of the camp near a ravine. There the troopers discovered a Mexican, long a Cheyenne captive, holding a baby. Clark watched as he handed the child to a trooper and was shot in the back as they forced him to run away down the ravine. Elliott then turned his field glasses to the trees downstream and spotted movement, mostly young boys according to Clark. "'There's a lot of escaping Indians; come on boys, let's take 'em in,'" Clark quoted Elliott and added, "The men who joined him did so of their own accord. The party rode away, but I did not follow. Men and horses soon disappeared in the timber."[29]

Out of sight and sound of Black Kettle's camp, Elliott and his volunteers ran into the Indian reinforcements coming upstream. At the same time, a large number of fugitives from Black Kettle's camp came up from the other direction. Elliott was suddenly caught be-

28 Charles J. Brill, "The End of the Cheyenne Trail," *The Daily Oklahoman* (Oklahoma City, Oklahoma), November 23, 1930.

29 "Custer's Washita Fight," *New York Sun*, May 14, 1899.

tween the Washita River and the creek with two groups of enemies converging on him. Cut off from help, Elliott made the mistake of having his men dismount and lie down in a circle facing outward. In the tall grass and below the banks, they lost their field of fire, but were exposed to enemy fire.[30]

By then Comanches from the camps downstream had joined the Indian reinforcements. Carney Saupitty, a great-grandson of eyewitness Kaywichamy, repeated his ancestor's account of what happened: "They come out from their campsite and they head for that Elliott's bunch. My great-grandfather, when they got near [the soldiers] was on horses, and he said that the commander talked real loud. He said they dismounted . . . and they all laid in a defensive [circle]. . . ." Putuaputiquay (One Who Looks after His Son) and Napiwatah (No Foot) rode in a circle around the prone soldiers. "They went round, and drawn the fire of those prone Elliott's division," Saupitty continued. "They didn't shoot, they were just makin' a circle. They were doin' that while everybody was coming toward that circle of men." A Cheyenne or Arapaho warrior, according to Kaywichamy, "rode his horse right up to them soldiers."[31] Later the Indians found the body of the warrior lying among the dead troopers.[32] Outnumbered and exposed, the soldiers had all been killed within an hour. The Cheyenne women stripped and mutilated their bodies to make their spirits harmless and piled them up like cordwood. Kaywichamy, according to Saupitty, said, "I looked there . . . and looked like they were on fire . . . but it was steam," rising straight up from the still-warm bodies in the cold, windless morning.[33]

Unaware of what was happening to Elliott and his volunteers and with Black Kettle's camp taken, Custer ordered the destruction of "everything of value to the Indians." This included, according to Custer, fifty-one lodges, all Cheyenne except for two that were Arapaho and two that were Sioux. In the lodges, the troopers sifted through Cheyenne belongings, turning up evidence of recent raids in Kansas: letters, daguerreotypes, and household goods. Custer's report enumerated 241 saddles, some highly decorated, 573 buffalo robes, 390 tanned tepee hides, 160 other hides, 210 axes, 140 hatchets, 35 revolvers, 47 rifles, 535 pounds of powder, 1,050 pounds of lead, 4000 arrows and arrow heads, 75 spears, 90 bullet moulds, 35 bows and quivers, 12 shields, 300 pounds of bullets, 775 lariats, 940 saddlebags, 470 blankets, 93 coats, 700 pounds of tobacco, and all the Cheyennes' winter provisions—dried meat, meal, and flour. From the estimated 875 horses and mules captured, some were set aside for transporting the fifty-three captive women and children. According to Clark, Custer gave the Osage trailers about fifty horses, while he picked our four of the best mules for himself, and allowed his officers to choose others, about 100 all together.[34]

30 Nye, *Carbine and Lance*, 67.

31 Interview of Carney Saupitty, Sr., by Mary Jane Warde, Lawton, Oklahoma, March 12, 1999, in Warde, *Final Report, Phase I.*

32 The Indian was probably an Arapaho named Smokey, or Tobacco. Nye, *Carbine and Lance*, 68.

33 Interview of Carney Saupitty, Sr., by Mary Jane Warde, Lawton, Oklahoma, March 12, 1999, in Warde, *Final Report, Phase I.*

34 Nye, *Carbine and Lance*, 68; Custer to Sheridan, November 28, 1868, 28; interview of Ben Clarke, 17.

Custer then ordered the rest of the horses to be rounded up and slaughtered. Moving Behind saw this from her hiding place and said, "The Indian ponies that were left were driven toward the bottoms. Some horses would run back, and the soldiers would chase them and head them the other way. Before leaving, the soldiers shot all the Indian ponies which they had driven to the bottoms."[35] Clark estimated that some 800 "were bunched up against the steep bank south of the village and two troops were detailed to kill them. One troop stood above the herd and the other in the valley below. It took nearly two hours to kill the ponies."[36]

By noon Custer was aware that there were many other Indians in the vicinity. Lt. E. S. Godfrey and a platoon, after rounding up the ponies, followed fleeing Cheyennes east along the north bank of the Washita River about two miles. As he topped a rise, he saw hundreds of lodges in the valley downstream. At the same time, Indians in the camps spotted him and charged in his direction. Godfrey and his platoon fought a running battle back to Black Kettle's camp. Along the way he heard heavy firing in the timber south of the river where Elliott was under attack, but he could not see what was happening. Godfrey reported that to Custer and questioned whether Elliott, who had not been seen for a while, might be involved in a fight. Custer said he did not think so.[37]

Meanwhile, the reinforcements from the other Indian camps had come into view. Clark said, "The hills appeared to be alive with them." They were armed with bows, arrows, shields, and guns and painted for the fight. "They had captured the overcoats of the sharpshooters, which had been left in the rear when the soldiers advanced to the fight. This pleased the Indians hugely," Clark said, "and they dared the soldiers to come and get them."[38] The burning of the camp and the slaughter of the horses infuriated them. Magpie, watching from the top of a high ridge, witnessed the destruction of his camp and pony herd. "This made the Indians very angry," he remembered, "and they would have attacked the soldiers had they not been afraid that such an attack would bring death to the women and children the soldiers had captured and were holding in the village."[39]

Custer watched the ever-growing number of hostile Indians uneasily. He sent Major Berry out with pickets to drive them back and hold them off because those with long-range rifles were already shooting into the camp. About mid-afternoon Custer took stock: Capt. Louis M. Hamilton was dead, shot through the heart in the first charge. Col. Albert Barnitz had taken a wound that appeared mortal. There were other minor wounds, but more troubling was the disappearance of Major Elliott and nineteen enlisted men. Ammunition was running low, the day was advancing, and their enemies were increasing, while Custer's troops were exhausted and hungry. Quar-

[35] Ediger and Hoffman, "Reminiscences," 139–140.

[36] "Custer's Washita Fight."

[37] Nye, *Carbine and Lance*, 68–69.

[38] Ibid.

[39] Brill, "End of the Cheyenne Trail."

Figure 8. Artist J. E. Taylor's depiction of the Washita Massacre appeared within a few years of the event. *Oklahoma Historical Society*

termaster James Bell was believed to be far back by the Antelope Hills with the supply wagons. His sudden dramatic arrival with fresh supplies of ammunition was an unexpected relief, but it was clearly time to withdraw. Late in the afternoon, Custer, still uncertain of Elliott's fate, collected his troops, his fifty-three prisoners, and captured livestock and moved downstream as if he intended to attack the other camps. It was a ruse. As the light faded, the column swung abruptly north and headed toward Camp Supply, not stopping until midnight.[40]

Moving Behind and her aunt stayed hidden in the weeds until late in the day when quiet returned to the river valley. When they dared poke their heads up, they saw Indian men and boys gathering along the riverbank and debating whether to follow the soldiers. Among them were Scabby, Afraid of Beaver, Roll Down, and others they knew. "While we stood there," Moving Behind remembered, "some young men rode up, and one of them recognized me as his girl friend. He got off, and as he shook hands with me, he asked, 'Is this you, Moving Behind?' I said, 'Yes.' We both cried, and hugged and

[40] Nye, *Carbine and Lance*, 69; Custer to Sheridan, November 28, 1868, 28–29.

kissed each other. This young man, named Crane, was my sweetheart in the good old days when I was young."[41]

Magpie rode down to the river with the small group of survivors and found the bodies of Black Kettle and Medicine Woman Later lying in the water next to their dead horse.[42] Clown, Afraid of Beaver, Scabby, and Roll Down brought the bodies out of the water and wrapped them in a red and blue blanket. Moving Behind said, "It was getting late, and we had to go, so we left the bodies of Black Kettle and his wife. As we rode westward, we would come across the bodies of men, women, and children, strewn about. We would stop and look at the bodies, and mention their names."[43]

Custer, the Seventh Cavalry troops, the prisoners, and the Osage trailers made a triumphal entrance into Camp Supply, but scouts who had kept an eye on the Indians had reported the deaths of Elliott and his volunteers. More than ten days passed before General Sheridan reached the killing ground and had the dead soldiers buried.[44]

In assessing the fight, two very different perspectives emerged from those who were there. Moving Behind was about eighty years old when she told an interviewer, "I have lived all these years, and before this no one has ever asked me to tell the story about how the soldiers approached the Black Kettle camp one morning at daybreak." She said, "I was there, and know what happened to us that morning, about dawn. That was where Black Kettle was killed, as well as many other Cheyennes."[45] In 1930 Magpie said, "They . . . tell me Custer said he killed 103 braves; but he did not. Only about 15 or 20 of our men were killed. All the others killed were women and children."[46] Custer, however, reported a great victory at the "battle of the Washita," and a great deal of positive publicity followed. Praising the perseverance and dedication of his troops, Custer's field report declared that his officers and men had "endured every privation and fought with unsurpassed gallantry against a powerful and well-armed foe. . . ."[47]

[41] Ediger and Hoffman, "Reminiscences," 140.

[42] Brill, "End of the Cheyenne Trail."

[43] Ediger and Hoffman, "Reminiscences," 140.

[44] Nye, *Carbine and Lance*, 70.

[45] Ediger and Hoffman, "Reminiscences," 137.

[46] Brill, "End of the Cheyenne Trail."

[47] Custer to Sheridan, November 28, 1868, 29.

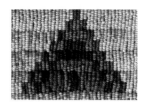

Chapter 2

A PLACE WELL KNOWN

Why did the Washita Massacre occur where it did—in today's Roger Mills County, Oklahoma? Over the centuries, the upper Washita River Valley has seen a succession of different peoples pass through, use, and live on the land. People have perceived the place in many ways, some of which can never be known but which were probably based on their association with it. The Cheyenne Indians called the Washita River the "Lodge (or Tepee) Pole River," because they camped there often and left their long tepee poles leaning against the trees between visits. The Comanche Indians called it "Buffalo Creek," and the Spanish called it the "Rio Negro," or Black River. The French called it the "False Washita" to distinguish it from the Ouachita River they had encountered farther east. Often, people moving into the region found others already there, using its resources. Sometimes those encounters were friendly, but sometimes they were not.[1]

The physical environment contributed to how people thought of and used the land. Roger Mills County in western Oklahoma is situated on the eastern edge of the High Plains, which extend into the neighboring Texas Panhandle. The land rises gradually toward the Rocky Mountains to the west or slopes eastward down to the distant Mississippi River. The Canadian River, which creates the northern boundary of the county, flows generally eastward across Oklahoma to join the Arkansas River. However, the Washita River and the North Fork of the Red River to the south curve east and then south to flow into the Red River. The country near Washita Battlefield is often rough and broken by creeks, but there are also level flood plains. Striking red hills surround Washita Battlefield. About twenty miles north, the Canadian River, which parallels the Washita River, loops around the Antelope Hills, five prominent gypsum-striped mesas. Across the county mixed-grass prairie to the east gives way to short-grass prairie to the west. Along the rivers and streams are ribbons of timber, much less now than in the past (See Map 3).[2]

The resources that first drew various people to the Washita River Valley over the centuries were those of this savannah and woodland setting: grasslands, water, game animals, fertile valleys,

[1] Interview of Laird Cometsevah, by Loretta Fowler, Clinton, Oklahoma, March 30, 2001 in Loretta Fowler, *Final Report, Ethnographic Overview (Phase II) for Washita Battlefield National Historic Site*, Cooperative Agreement No. 1443CA125098002 (Modification 3), National Park Service, June 26, 2001, 105; "Map of the Country Drained by the Mississippi" in "Part III of James's Account of S. H. Long's Expedition, 1819–1820" in *Early Western Travels, 1748– 1846*, vol. 16, ed. Reuben Gold Thwaites (Cleveland: Arthur H. Clark Company, 1905).

[2] See various maps in John W. Morris, Charles R. Goins, and Edwin C. McReynolds, *Historical Atlas of Oklahoma* (Norman: University of Oklahoma Press, 1965, 1986 edition).

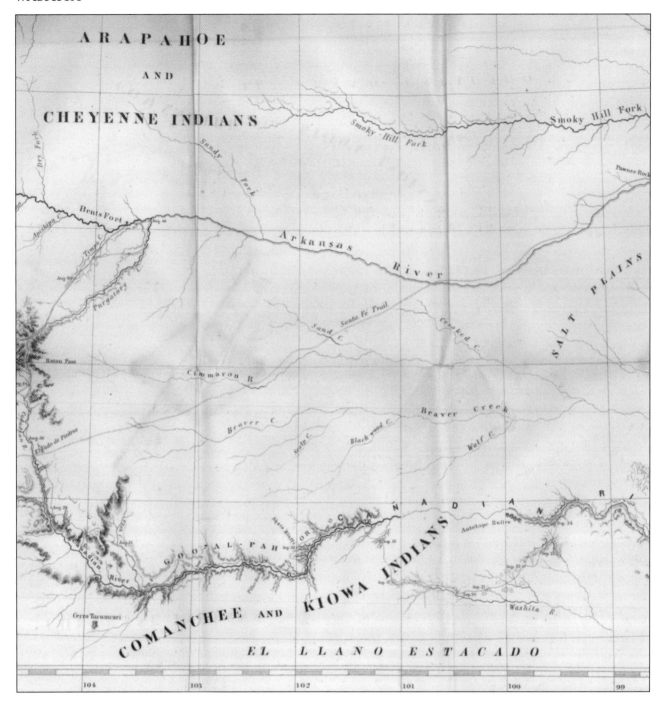

Map 3. This portion of Abert's map shows his return route east along the Washita and Canadian rivers as well as the ranges of the Cheyennes, Arapahos, Kiowas, and Comanches in the early 1800s.[3]

timber, and useful plants. Prehistoric and historic Indian hunters and farmers preceded nomadic Plains tribes into the Washita River Valley near Washita Battlefield. In 2000, surveys had identified more than 900 archaeological sites in Roger Mills County alone. Archaeologists have discovered traces of villages they classify as the

Figure 9. Ancestors of the Wichita Indians are believed to have lived in the Washita River Valley as early as 800 A.D. The grass house is a typical Wichita dwelling. *Oklahoma Historical Society*

Custer Phase in the upper Washita River Valley and the Canadian River Valley. They are thought to date from 800 to 1450 A.D. The people who lived in these clusters of rectangular houses raised maize, beans, and squash, collected other food plants, and hunted bison.

About 1250 to 1450, people of the Turkey Creek Phase also farmed but had increased their dependence on bison hunting. However, about 1500 the population level in the villages declined as, it is thought, the inhabitants moved north toward the Arkansas River Valley. Even then, their hunters may have returned to the Washita and Canadian river valleys to kill bison. Some archaeologists believe that these people were ancestors of the Wichita Indians, a Caddoan people who still lived along Oklahoma's river systems when Europeans entered the region. Today they are the Wichita and Affiliated Tribes, with their headquarters just north of the Washita River at Anadarko, Oklahoma. [4]

By the late fifteenth or early sixteenth centuries, Lipan Apaches, an Athapascan group, had moved from the Rocky Mountains onto the Southern Plains. The Antelope Hills served as a frequent rendezvous for nomadic bands hunting bison in the area.[5] Alonzo Chalepah of today's Apache Tribe of Oklahoma described the nearby Washita River Valley as "a stopping point to camp because of the environment that supplied them . . . water and hunting and game and fowl, etc." They collected "whatever may be ripened at that time, be it berries, roots, nuts or whatever."[6]

It was along the Canadian River in the Texas Panhandle west of the Antelope Hills that the first Europeans known to be in the vicinity of Washita Battlefield National Historic Site encountered the

[3] "Map Showing the Route Pursued by the Exploring Expedition to New Mexico and the Southern Rocky Mountains Made under the Orders of Captain J. C. Fremont, U.S. Topographical Engineers and Conducted by Lieut. J. W. Abert, Assisted by Lieut. W. G. Peck, V .S. T .E., during the Year 1845," in J. W. Abert, "Report," *Message from the President of the United States*, 29th Cong., 1st sess., S. Doc. 438, Oklahoma Historical Society, Oklahoma City, Oklahoma.

[4] Lee Bement and Kent Buehler, "Bison, Nuts, and the Dempsey Divide," *Oklahoma Archaeological Survey Newsletter* 20 (July 2000):1; Richard R. Drass, "The Southern Plains Villagers," in *Archaeology in the Great Plains*, ed. W. Raymond Wood (Lawrence: University Press of Kansas, 1998), 427–441; Susan C. Vehik, "Cultural Continuity and Discontinuity in the Southern Prairies and Cross Timbers," ibid., 242–245.

[5] W. David Baird and Danney Goble, *The Story of Oklahoma* (Norman: University of Oklahoma Press Press, 1994), 60.

[6] Interview of Alonzo Chalepah, by Loretta Fowler, Anadarko, Oklahoma, March 31, 2003, in Loretta Fowler, *Draft Report, Phase III for Washita Battlefield National Historic Site*, Cooperative Agreement No. 1443CA125098002 (Modification 4), National Park Service, March 27, 2003.

Figure 10. Spanish explorers visited Apache camps similar to this one near the Antelope Hills. Descendants of these Indians are the Apache Tribe of Oklahoma. *Oklahoma Historical Society*

Apaches. Francisco Vasquez de Coronado had come through the region in 1541, following rumors of rich cities such as those the Spanish had recently conquered in Mexico. It is not known for sure just where Coronado crossed western Oklahoma on his way northeastward into Kansas. He did not find the rich kingdom he looked for, but periodically other Spanish explorers ventured onto the Southern Plains in search of wealth. They also wanted to secure Spain's hold on its northern frontier, then the New Mexico colony.[7] In 1601 Gov. Juan de Onate followed the Canadian River, the "Rio de Magdalena," which rises in eastern New Mexico, toward what he hoped was the kingdom of Quivira. His party included two Franciscan friars, seventy picked men, a herd of 700 horses and mules, six carts, four artillery pieces, and servants. Somewhere in the Texas Panhandle, the expedition encountered the Apaches, called by the expedition chronicler "the masters of the plains." He described how they greeted the Spanish peacefully and brought gifts of small, tasty fruit. "They have no permanent settlements or homes," he wrote, "but follow the cattle [bison] as they roam about. We had no trouble with them, even though we crossed their land, nor was there an Indian who ventured to harm us in the least. . . ."[8]

But even more impressive to the Spanish than the Indians were the bison. The chronicler wrote, ". . . We found so many of them that it will be difficult for anyone who has not seen them to believe it. . . . They were so tame that unless chased or frightened they stood still and did not run away." Noting the animals' hump-backed bodies, short legs, and thick hair, the chronicler continued, "Their shape is so amazing that one cannot help but believe that it is the result of the crossing of different animals." He concluded with the observation, ". . . The Indians are skillful in dressing the skins and making

[7] Morris, Goins, and McReynolds, *Historical Atlas*, Map 11.

[8] George P. Hammond and Agapito Rey, *Don Juan de Onate: Colonizer of New Mexico, 1595–1628* (n.p.: University of New Mexico Press, 1953), 749.

them into clothes."[9] Near the Antelope Hills, Onate turned northeast toward the Wichita villages on the Arkansas River close to present Wichita, Kansas. Conflict with the Apaches may have been one reason the Wichitas had moved there, but the Apaches, too, eventually moved deep into Texas for safety, abandoning the vicinity of Washita Battlefield for the time being.[10]

Alonzo Baca retraced Onate's route through western Oklahoma in 1634. The failure of these two early expeditions to find wealthy cities northeast of New Mexico ended official Spanish exploration of western Oklahoma for almost a century. However, it did strengthen the claim of Spain on the region at a time during which European colonizers were turning their attention to the interior of the North American continent.[11]

The advent of European explorers and traders transformed the cultures of the Great Plains tribes and eventually the population around Washita Battlefield. The introduction of European trade goods—including firearms—and horses upset the balance of power among enemies, made some peoples more much more mobile, allowed greater dependence on bison hunting, and diminished the importance of farming among some tribes. A prime example were the Comanches, who acquired horses by 1700 and moved onto the Great Plains from the northern Rocky Mountains to become bison hunters, excellent horsemen, and superior horse raiders. The Cheyennes, an Algonkian people, also experienced great cultural change about the same time. In 1673 Cheyennes lived in earth lodges, farmed, and hunted in northern Minnesota, but they moved into South Dakota to escape intertribal conflict stemming from the European/Indian fur trade. Their migration continued through the 1700s as they acquired horses and gave up farming for bison hunting. By the early 1800s they had reached the Platte River and formed an alliance with the Arapahos. Accomplished bison hunters and horsemen, the Arapahos, also Algonkian, usually ranged ahead of the Cheyennes, moving as far south as the Arkansas River. Meanwhile, the Osages, who lived east of the Mississippi River until the late 1600s, used firearms traded from the French to establish themselves as a force in the lower Missouri River Valley. Eventually they laid claim to hunting grounds in present Missouri, Kansas, and Oklahoma. Among those who suffered from increasing Osage aggressiveness were the Wichitas, then situated along the middle Arkansas River Valley. By the 1700s the Canadian River Valley marked a neutral zone between the Osages and the Comanche Indians. When parties from the two tribes visited the Canadian and Washita rivers to hunt, chance encounters were likely to result in violence.[12]

The French ventured into this fluid situation on the Southern Plains in the early 1700s by way of the Arkansas River Valley in to-

[9] Ibid., 749–750.

[10] Ibid., 750.

[11] Grant Foreman, "Early Trails through Oklahoma," *The Chronicles of Oklahoma* 3 (June 1925):100; A. B. Thomas, "Spanish Exploration of Oklahoma, 1599–1792," *The Chronicles of Oklahoma* 6 (June 1928): 190–195.

[12] Arrell Morgan Gibson, *The American Indian: Prehistory* to *the Present* (Norman: University of Oklahoma Press, 1980), 241–245; Donald J. Berthrong, *The Southern Cheyennes* (Norman: University of Oklahoma Press, 1963), 10–13; Fowler, *Final Report, Phase II*, 12–14; Arrell Morgan Gibson, *Oklahoma: A History of Five Centuries* (Norman: University of Oklahoma Press, 1965, 1981 edition), 24; Willard H. Rollings, *The Osage: An Ethnohistorical Study of Hegemony on the Prairie Plains* (Columbia: University of Missouri Press, 1992), 147.

Figure 11. Once Cheyennes became bison hunters, they exchanged the earth lodge for the tepee and lived in camps such as this one. *Oklahoma Historical Society*

day's eastern Oklahoma. Although the French did not officially enter the upper Washita River Valley, they claimed the region as part of their "Louisiana" colony. A major French goal was opening trade between Louisiana and Spanish Santa Fe, but Spain's restrictive colonial trade policies usually blocked the way. In 1739–1740, improved French relations among the Plains tribes allowed brothers Pierre and Paul Mallet to go to New Mexico by way of the Platte River. They returned east down the Canadian River, passing through present Roger Mills County, to French posts along the Arkansas River. The financial success of their venture encouraged further exploration of the Canadian River, or the "St. Andre," as the most direct route to New Mexico. But, discouraged by the sand bars and shallow water, later French expeditions traveling by canoe turned back far downstream. The Mallet brothers had, however, discovered the advantage that in the future drew more Euro-Americans to the region of Washita Battlefield: The narrow divide between the Washita River and the Canadian River provided a natural east-west passage across the Southern Plains.[13]

Although the French never succeeded in opening trade with Santa Fe, they did accomplish their second goal: extending their Indian fur trade to the Plains tribes. By the time the Mallet brothers

[13] Morris, Goins, and McReynolds, *Historical Atlas*, Map 13; Gibson, *Oklahoma*, 20–21.

Figure 12. The Washita River Valley was rich in bison and other game animals. Plains Indians such as these Kiowas traded bison robes to the French for European goods. *Oklahoma Historical Society*

made their trip to Santa Fe, French traders and trappers enjoyed a good trade relationship with the Wichitas. As their ancestors had for centuries, they still lived in grass houses, farmed the river valleys across Oklahoma, and produced a surplus of food. Stuart Owings, a Wichita, explained,

> . . . They would take all their dried goods, all their meat and squash and corn, peas, whatever they had, whatever they grew, and they would dig caches or holes along rivers or creeks and they would put grass down and leaves, and put their layer of vegetables and put some more leaves and limbs down, and put some more layers to be able to keep the vegetables that way. But, of course, a lot of the different tribes that didn't grow—the Kiowas and Comanches—would ride up and down the creeks or rivers and find out where those caches were and dig them up. Cache, Oklahoma and Cache Creek, that's what they were named after, those caches of food that they would put along there.[14]

In 1740 the Wichitas and Comanches formed an alliance based on trade. The Wichitas exchanged their surplus corn, beans, squash, gourds, and tobacco with French traders for firearms, iron pots, needles, beads, and paint. The Wichitas then traded these European

[14] Interview of Stuart Owings, by Loretta Fowler, Anadarko, Oklahoma, November 8, 2002, in Fowler, *Draft Report, Phase III.*

goods, along with surplus crops, to the Comanches for their bison robes and the horses and slaves they captured in New Mexico and other Spanish provinces. French traders would then take these Indian goods and captives down the Arkansas River for re-sale. Late in the 1700s the Southern Plains alliance extended even further. Kiowas and Apaches (the latter descendants of the Apaches Onate encountered near the Antelope Hills) moved into the region. Although enmity had existed between the Kiowas and Comanches since both lived near the Black Hills in South Dakota, in 1790 Guikate, second chief of the Kiowas, negotiated a peace that ended Kiowa/Comanche friction. Thereafter, the Kiowas participated in Wichita trade, and the Comanches, Kiowas, and Apaches often camped together and shared the resources of western Oklahoma in a peace that has never been broken.[15]

While the French, Wichitas, Comanches, Kiowas, and Apaches benefitted from their trade alliances, others opposed them. The Osages, expanding southwest from the Missouri River Valley and well armed through French trade, claimed much of the central Plains, including most of present Oklahoma and its resources. This resulted in clashes with the Apaches, Comanches, and Kiowas, most notably the 1833 Cut-Throat Gap Massacre in the Wichita Mountains about eighty miles southeast of Washita Battlefield. By the 1740s Osage raids forced the Wichitas to move south from the Arkansas River Valley to the safety of the Red River Valley. At their fortified villages on either side of the Red River near today's Ryan, Oklahoma, they continued their profitable trade. However, Spanish colonial policy prohibited trading firearms to Indians, particularly the Comanches, who plagued their settlements in New Mexico and Texas. This, along with Comanche/Wichita attacks on Texas missions, led in 1759 to a large but unsuccessful Spanish expedition against the Wichita villages on the Red River. The Wichitas maintained their position as middlemen between the French and the Southern Plains tribes in the region of Washita Battlefield until 1763. Then at the end of the Seven Years' (French and Indian) War, France transferred Louisiana to Spain. Cut off from their supply of European goods, the Wichitas grew poor as they lost control of Southern Plains trade.[16]

The transfer of Louisiana to Spain in 1763 included the Washita and Canadian river valleys. Attempts to link Santa Fe commercially to formerly-French St. Louis resulted in renewed official interest in Southern Plains trade routes along the river valleys. There is no conclusive proof of Spanish presence near Washita Battlefield during this period. Unofficially, however, New Mexicans ventured routinely into the region. Large parties of *ciboleros* hunted bison for meat and hides along the Canadian River for two centuries, beginning in

15 Gibson, *Oklahoma*, 21–25; James Mooney, "Calendar History of the Kiowa," *Seventeenth Annual Report of the Bureau of American Ethnology, 1895–1896*, vol. 17, pt. 1 (Washington: Government Printing Office, 1898):162–165; Mildred P. Mayhall, *The Kiowas* Norman: University of Oklahoma Press, 1962), 12–13.

16 Gibson, *Oklahoma*, 26, 55. At Cut-Throat Gap near present Roosevelt, Oklahoma, Osages attacked a Kiowa camp and cut off the heads of their victims, an Osage warning against hunting in their territory. See John Joseph Mathews, *The Osages: Children of the Middle Waters* (Norman: University of Oklahoma Press, 1961), 553–557, and James Mooney, *Calendar History of the Kiowa Indians* (Washington, D.C.: Smithsonian Institution Press, 1979), 257–269, 318.

Figure 13. Artist George Catlin sketched this Comanche camp in western Oklahoma in the 1830s.
Oklahoma Historical Society

the late 1600s. About 1800, New Mexican *comancheros* established trade with the Comanche Indians, traveling as far as the Wichita Mountains about eighty miles southeast of Washita Battlefield. About twenty-five miles south of Washita Battlefield, the heavy wheels of New Mexican carts carved a deeply rutted road along the North Fork of the Red River as they traveled between Santa Fe and the Spanish settlements at present Natchitoches, Louisiana, and Nacogdoches, Texas. It is safe to say, then, that New Mexicans knew the region and its resources long before the arrival of Anglo-Americans in the early 1800s.[17]

The transfer of Louisiana back to France during the Napoleonic Wars and then to the United States in the 1803 Louisiana Purchase had little impact on the native inhabitants of the Washita Battlefield area. What was probably more important to them was the continuing flux as other tribes migrated into the area. The 1790 peace created by the Kiowas and Comanches continued. However, a generation later incursions of Cheyennes and Arapahos, moving in from the north, threatened stability. By the early 1800s, they had reached the headwaters of the Arkansas River, still some distance from the Kiowas, Apaches, and Comanches, who generally camped between the Canadian River and the North Fork of the Red River. As late as 1821 relations among the five tribes were good, but by 1826 the Cheyennes were routinely raiding Kiowa and Comanche horse herds, taking as many as one thousand head at a time. Among

[17] Scholars differ over whether Pedro Vial traversed the area in 1792 or followed a more westerly route. See for example, Thomas, "Spanish Exploration of Oklahoma," 197, 211–212, and Noel M. Loomis and Abraham P. Nasatir, *Pedro Vial and the Roads to Santa Fe* (Norman: University of Oklahoma Press, 1967), 266. Grant Foreman, "Early Trails through Oklahoma," *The Chronicles of Oklahoma* 3 (June 1925):100–110; "Ciboleros" and "Comancheros," in Handbook of Texas Online, retrieved February 6, 2002, from www.tsha.utexas.edu/handbook/online; INTERNET.

the Plains tribes, horse raiding had become an important way for a man to accumulate wealth and status, while he proved himself as a leader. It has been said that the Pawnees from Nebraska stole horses from the Cheyennes, who stole them from the Kiowas and Comanches, who stole them from the New Mexicans in the first place.[18]

A horse raid by Cheyennes in 1837 led to the final confrontation between the two competing alliances of Southern Plains tribes. Kiowas, the intended victims of the horse raid, and Comanches camped nearby killed the entire raiding party—thirty-eight Bowstring Warrior Society members and four Contraries—that had targeted their Sun Dance encampment. When word reached the Cheyennes of the deaths that fall, all ten Cheyenne bands and the Arapahos planned a retaliatory expedition against the Kiowas for the summer of 1838. On June 23, somewhere along Wolf Creek, about fifty miles north of Washita Battlefield, the combined Cheyenne and Arapaho tribes attacked the Sun Dance encampment of Kiowas, Apaches, and Comanches. After a day of heavy fighting with substantial losses on both sides, the Cheyennes and Arapahos withdrew, and the Kiowas chose not to follow them. The two alliances had tested each other at full strength with neither emerging as the victor. Two years later, in 1840, after a smallpox epidemic devastated the Plains Indians, the five tribes made peace at a large gathering on the Arkansas River three miles downstream from Bent's Fort in Colorado. Thereafter, they often fought together, camped together, and defended each other as they did during the Washita Massacre at Washita Battlefield.[19]

One can speculate that one reason they were willing to make peace among themselves was that they faced increasing encroachment from Anglo-Americans in the early decades of the 1800s. The Anglo-American settler frontier still lay fairly far to the east, but already there was a line of new states west of the Mississippi River. Trappers and traders were making their way up the western rivers into the Rocky Mountains to trap beaver. Moreover, with Mexican independence from Spain won in 1821, adventurous merchants were taking caravans loaded with trade goods over the Santa Fe Trail through the lands claimed by the five Southern Plains tribes. As Plains Indians looked eastward, it must have seemed that an ominous cloud lay along the horizon.

[18] Mary Jane Warde, "Alternative Perspectives on the Battle of Wolf Creek of 1838," *Indigenous Nations Studies Journal* 2 (Fall 2001):3–4.

[19] Ibid., 4–10.

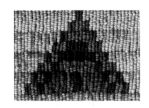

Chapter 3

A DIFFERENT ROAD

By the early 1800s, a more or less standard pattern of Anglo-American frontier development had been established. Soon after the end of the War of 1812, Anglo-Americans were planting farms and trading posts in what became eastern Oklahoma. Eventually they might have moved onto the prairies west of the Cross Timbers, the belt of timber that stretches across today's Oklahoma from Kansas to Texas and separates the eastern woodlands from the Great Plains. However, by 1830 federal policy had dictated a different road for what became Oklahoma, including the area around Washita Battlefield.

Even before traders packed their goods and headed for Santa Fe in 1821, the federal government had ordered a series of surveying expeditions to inventory the resources of its western lands and locate potential routes across the Great Plains. One of the first surveyors was Maj. Stephen Long, who had earlier explored the U.S./Spanish boundary and selected the site for the construction of Fort Smith, Arkansas. Long, accompanied by botanist Edwin James and artist Titian Peale, was ordered to locate the headwaters of the Platte and Arkansas rivers near the Rocky Mountains and to return east along the Red River. Reaching the mouth of the Washita River, which empties into the Red River, would be a milestone on the return trip. Unfortunately, Long's party picked up the Canadian River instead of the Red River and followed it east. As far as his Comanche and Kiowa guides were concerned, the "Gooalpah"—the Kiowa name for the Canadian—*was* the "red river."[1]

This first official federal surveying party in the vicinity of Washita Battlefield crossed the 100th meridian into Roger Mills County near the Antelope Hills on August 17, 1821. In the late summer heat, the grass was brown and the Canadian River was low, offering little water except in shallow, stagnant pools. But herds of bison cows grazed nearby, promising good fresh meat, and the elm trees in a small valley southwest of the river were covered in wild grape vines heavy with fruit. After days of heat, thirst, and short rations, botanist James rhapsodized about this find: "Here are hundreds of acres, covered with a movable surface of sand, and abounding in vines. . . ." The sun and wind had pruned them naturally, max-

[1] See William H. Goetzmann, *Army Exploration in the American West, 1803–1863* (New Haven: Yale University Press, 1959), and James Smallwood, "Major Stephen Harriman Long, 1820," in *Frontier Adventurers: American Exploration* in *Oklahoma,* ed. Joseph A. Stout, Jr. (Oklahoma City: Oklahoma Historical Society, 1976), 51–57.

Figure 14. The Antelope Hills as seen by Abert and his party in 1845. *Oklahoma Historical Society*

imizing the production of grapes. "We indulged ourselves to excess," James wrote, ". . . and invited by the cleanness of the sand, and a refreshing shade, we threw ourselves down, and slept away, with unusual zest, a few of the hours of a summer afternoon."[2]

The botanist described a region empty of human inhabitants but crisscrossed with well-defined animal trails—all leading to the nearest water source. There were "astonishing numbers of bison, deer, antelopes,"[3] and other grazing animals as well as the wolves and coyotes that preyed on them. Black bears and turkeys shared the wild grapes and plums found in the ravines. Red sandstone outcroppings striped with gypsum, fine-grained red soil, plentiful springs, and close-cropped grasses were the most obvious features on the landscape. James speculated that the presence of black walnut trees meant the soil could support agriculture, but its sandiness prevented the retention of water. However, if one burned off the native grasses and sowed domestic grasses, he believed, grazing might be improved for livestock production. In spite of James's optimistic conclusions, Long's report describing the relatively empty Texas Panhandle and western Oklahoma as a "desert" contributed to Anglo-American public perception of it as an inhospitable land, a view Indian people did not share.[4]

Not until 1840, two decades later, did another Anglo-American document his views of the Washita Battlefield vicinity. Josiah Gregg, a scholarly man with an adventurous spirit, believed that the French blockade of Vera Cruz in 1839 offered the opportunity for a

[2] Thomas James, "S. H. Long's Expedition," in *Early Western Travels*, vol. 16, ed. Thwaites, 134.

[3] Ibid., 140.

[4] Ibid., 133–145; Smallwood, "Long," 60.

merchant to profit by freighting goods overland to isolated Santa Fe. In April 1839 Gregg led a party of traders westward from Van Buren, Arkansas, to the lower Canadian River, out along its valley, and then across the 100th meridian by a northerly route through present Woodward County, Oklahoma. The following spring, they returned more directly via the Canadian River, crossing into today's Oklahoma at the "Boundary Mountains," or the Antelope Hills, on March 25. Leading them was a Comanche guide as well as several New Mexicans, who knew the country but believed the Washita River, or the "Rio Negro," was a tributary of the Canadian. Gregg's party—twenty-eight wagons, two hundred mules, and a herd of sheep and goats—kept to the narrow divide between the Canadian and the Washita, where tough prairie grasses prevented their wheels from sinking into the sandy soil. Although traveling through present Roger Mills and Dewey counties was relatively easy, the winter-dry grass posed a constant fire hazard. The party continued down the Canadian River to the vicinity of present Geary, Oklahoma, at which point they picked up their trail of the previous year. Gregg published his experiences in 1844 as *Commerce of the Prairies*. While the book contributed little to the Santa Fe trade, it provided important information to travelers seeking a fast and easy passage to California.[5]

Among his readers was Lt. James William Abert, a West Point graduate serving with the Army Corps of Topographical Engineers. In 1845 he was assigned to the third western exploration of Capt. John C. Fremont. However, while Fremont went on to California that summer, Abert and Lt. William G. Peck, guided by mountain man Thomas Fitzpatrick, led a party of thirty-three civilians southeastward from Bent's Fort through the Southern Plains Comanche and Kiowa country. Their route—a road much traveled by New Mexican carts, packhorses, and Indian ponies—paralleled the Canadian River, which Abert labeled the "Goo-al-pah" on his maps. It took them from New Mexico east across the arid tableland of the Texas Panhandle. Rather than follow Gregg's route along the Canadian River, they were to locate the headwaters of the Washita River, follow it downstream to the "sand hills," and then cross the divide back to the Canadian. They did so until the Washita coursed away from the Canadian east of the 101st meridian. Uncertain if they had reached the correct sand hills, they turned northeast, crossing the 100th meridian into Roger Mills County on September 21. Abert, used to the well-watered and well-timbered East, found the landscape, which was dotted by small hills topped with shin oaks, refreshing after the treeless and monotonous Staked Plain. Although the prairie grass was dry and brown that late in the season, the Abert party enjoyed ripe grapes, as had Long's expedition two decades earlier. Abert catalogued plants and many birds, including scissor-tailed

[5] James West, "Josiah Gregg, 1839–1840," in *Frontier Adventurers*, ed. Stout, 101–109; "Gregg's Commerce of the Prairies" in *Early Western Travels*, ed. Thwaites, 216–129; Morris, Goins, and McReynolds, *Historical Atlas*, Map 17.

Figure 15. The shallow Canadian River marked a major route across the Southern Plains. *Oklahoma Historical Society*

flycatchers, quail, prairie chickens, turkeys, and turkey buzzards as he noted signs indicating they were approaching the bison range. Numerous tepee rings demonstrated frequent occupation by Plains Indians they guessed were Comanches, reinforcing their conclusion that this was a good hunting ground and camping location. On September 23 they zigzagged their wagons northeastward around deep timbered ravines cut into red clay and gypsum stream banks, probably crossing Dead Indian Creek to camp near present Roll, Oklahoma. Then, on September 24, they again approached the Canadian River, its course identifiable by the haze of wind-blown sand hanging over the valley. They camped some twenty miles east of the Antelope Hills, but there was still another day of hard travel toward the present Roger Mills-Dewey county line. The sandy river bottom dragged at their wagon wheels, forcing them back up the heavily eroded escarpment to firmer ground. In mapping, sketching, and describing the region, Abert systematically reported on water sources (often bad), minerals, plants, and the abundant herds of bison and deer, as well as wild horses and the occasional panther and bear. But his reconnaissance had not revealed a route better than the one Gregg described along the Washita-Canadian divide.[6]

Five years later, as news of gold strikes in California galvanized the nation, Gen. Matthew Arbuckle, commander of Fort Smith in western Arkansas, also studied Gregg's *Commerce of the Prairies* for a good route west. At the time, 1849, the town surrounding Fort Smith was vying with neighboring Van Buren, Arkansas, to be the terminus of an overland route to the Pacific Coast. Arbuckle threw his support to the garrison town's boosters, and ordered Capt.

[6] Abert, "Report," 48–49, 52–60; Goetzmann, *Army Exploration*, 123–127.

Figure 16. Randolph Marcy led goldseekers west along the California Road and later surveyed the area for a possible transcontinental railroad route. *Oklahoma Historical Society*

Randolph B. Marcy to locate a route west from Fort Smith. An expedition of "Argonauts"—soldiers and California-bound civilians—set off in May by way of the Canadian River. Lt. James H. Simpson of the Topographical Corps accompanied Marcy as his assistant.[7]

Marcy's party enjoyed an uneventful trip along the south bank, sighting the Antelope Hills while still a full day's travel east. Hills and ravines—"thrown up without the slightest reference to finish or utility"—cut up the surface of present eastern Roger Mills County. On May 29 Marcy wrote, "I am convinced that the only place along near our route where a natural wagon road can be found is directly upon the crest of the Divide" between the Canadian and Washita rivers. Elaborating in the next day's journal entry, he wrote that the ridge, though often curving with the riverbed, was "very firm and smooth." Marcy declared, "I have never seen a better natural road. The country upon each side falling off towards the Canadian and Washita, leaves the crest perfectly dry at all seasons." Timber and grass-lined streams provided plenty of campsites, but, he added, "The soil is unfit for cultivation, being a hard gravelly sand, and very poor." On May 31 the Argonauts traveled across the prairie at the foot of the Antelope Hills, which Marcy took to be of volcanic origin. On June 1 they went fourteen miles farther, crossing the Texas line into a region of small lakes (perhaps buffalo wallows), prairie dog towns, and buffalo

7 W. Eugene Hollon, *Beyond the Cross Timbers: The Travels of Randolph B. Marcy, 1812–1887* (Norman: University of Oklahoma Press, 1955), 56–57; Goetzmann, *Army Exploration*, 213–217.

grass. Marcy wrote, "This grass is very short and thick; but animals are extravagantly fond of it, and it is very nutritious."[8]

Wood, water, and grass were the primary needs of nineteenth-century Southern Plains travelers, and the route described by Gregg and Marcy along the Canadian-Washita divide offered all three. However, Lieutenant Simpson, the expedition topographical officer, examined the route for possible railroad construction. He concluded that it had possibilities but lacked the centers of population necessary to develop the local resources and to make a railroad project feasible.[9]

Marcy's Argonauts were only one of many parties of immigrants making their way to the California gold fields over the Canadian-Washita River route, which soon became known as the "California Road." An immigrant who arrived too late that spring to travel with Marcy wrote to the *Baltimore Sun* that more than nine hundred wagons and two thousand people had already left Fort Smith on the California Road along the Canadian River. "There is no doubt," he stated, "this route will supercede all other land routes to Santa Fe and San Francisco, being the shortest, best watered and has the best grazing."[10]

Just a few years later, intensifying interest in railroad transportation sent Marcy back along the California Road, this time to examine the route from the perspective of the railroad builder. The federal government needed information about a possible route from the Mississippi River to the Pacific Coast near the 35th parallel. After traveling the route again in 1852, Marcy was still convinced that the Canadian River Valley and the Washita divide offered the best route west, one requiring minimal bridging and grading. Aided by George B. McClellan, brevet captain of engineers, he created a report that detailed watercourses, soil, grade, minerals, and vegetation. The following year Lt. Amiel Weeks Whipple traveled the California Road from Fort Smith to Albuquerque, New Mexico, participating in a series of surveys of the central United States aimed at finding a transcontinental railroad route. In a detailed report, illustrated by artist Heinrich Balduin Möllhausen, Whipple too noted the benefits of a route along the Washita-Canadian divide, particularly near the Antelope Hills. However, selecting the route and constructing the railroad became increasingly embroiled in the nation's sectional and political conflict toward the late 1850s.[11]

Even though railroads were assuming growing importance in transportation, there was still a need for good wagon roads that could accommodate the increasing volume of traffic bound for California. This was evident in 1858 when Edward F. Beale was hired to survey a wagon road from Fort Smith, Arkansas, to the Colorado River. In mild winter weather, the Beale party moved through western Okla-

[8] Grant Foreman, *Marcy and the Gold Seekers: The Journal of Captain R. B. Marcy, with an Account of the Gold Rush over the Southern Route* (Norman: University of Oklahoma Press, 1939), 216–220.

[9] Goetzmann, *Army Exploration*, 216–217.

[10] Foreman, *Marcy and the Gold Seekers*, 130n.

[11] Randolph B. Marcy, *Exploration of the Red River of Louisiana, in the Year 1852*, 33d Cong., 1st sess., H.R. Ex. Doc. (Washington, D.C.: A.O.P. Nicholson, Public Printer, 1854), 110–113; Amiel Weeks Whipple, "Report on the Topographical Features and Character of the Country," *Reports of Explorations and Surveys, to Ascertain the Most Practicable and Economical Route for a Railroad from the Mississippi River to the Pacific Ocean, 1853–4*, pt. 2, vol. 3, 33d Cong., 2d sess., S. Ex. Doc. 78, 1856, 12–14.

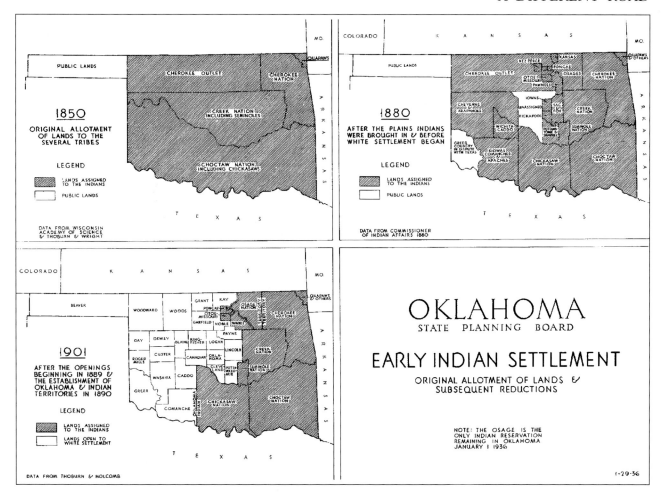

Map 4. Indian Territory in 1850 included almost all of today's Oklahoma. By 1901, as shown on these maps, the western half had already been divided into counties in preparation for statehood.[14]

homa over the route described earlier by Gregg, Marcy, and Whipple, bridging the streams as they went. F. E. Engle, who kept the expedition journal, concluded that this was "the best emigrant road between the frontier of the States and California."[12] Engle also foresaw a bright future for the area. Five days before the party passed out of Roger Mills County past the Antelope Hills, he described the valley near Washita Battlefield "the widest and most productive we have seen, and in time will afford homes to thousands who are now without them."[13]

However, the Beale expedition journal also reflected a concern that many who traveled the California Road shared. By the time they reached the vicinity of Washita Battlefield, they were entering the domain of the Kiowa and Comanche Indians. Although members of these tribes had provided information to earlier explorers and guided parties through the Texas Panhandle and western Oklahoma, they were now regarded as unpredictable and a potential threat. When

[12] Quoted in Grant Foreman, ed., "Survey of a Wagon Road from Fort Smith to the Colorado River," *The Chronicles of Oklahoma* 12 (March 1934):93.

[13] Ibid.

[14] Oklahoma State Planning Board, *Preliminary Report on State Planning, 1936* (Oklahoma City: State Capitol, 1936), 2.

Beale approached Black Beaver about guiding his party west, the famous Delaware scout warned him that the Comanches were hostile to white men and were likely to burn the prairie to deprive them of grass for their livestock. Beale's journalist Engle apparently took such warnings to heart: He suggested the California Road could be shortened by bridging several of the streams, but the bridges would have to be made of iron to prevent the Indians from burning them.[15]

In the normal course of Anglo-American frontier development, the tide of settlement might have moved along the California Road past Washita Battlefield with the soldiers, surveyors, traders, forty-niners, and travelers. However, the federal government intervened in the 1820s and 1830s with an Indian policy that channeled the flow of settlement elsewhere. To meet public demand, it urged and later required that all Indian people in the East move west of the Mississippi River, and Congress passed the Indian Removal Act (1830) to support the policy. A large area loosely labeled the "Indian Territory" became a new homeland for tribes forced to emigrate. Included was the upper Washita River Valley. This effectively eliminated the region and the valley from the general path of expanding nineteenth-century Anglo-American settlement.[16]

Instead, in 1830 by the Treaty of Dancing Rabbit Creek, the Choctaw Nation exchanged all its lands in the Southeast for new lands between the Canadian and Red rivers, a domain stretching from the Arkansas border to the 100th meridian. It included Washita Battlefield (See Map 4). Seven years later, the Chickasaws, their neighbors back east, purchased the right to settle in the new Choctaw country. The two tribes separated in 1855, and the Chickasaws moved into the middle third of the original Choctaw country, while retaining a one-quarter interest in the western third. To their north, the Muskogee (or Creek) Nation, Seminole Nation, and Cherokee Nation in the 1820s and 1830s purchased lands that extended from the borders of Arkansas and Kansas to the 100th meridian. Although hunting, trading, and diplomatic parties sometimes ventured far to the west within these boundaries, members of these nations generally preferred to live in the more familiar physical environment east of the Cross Timbers. Even so, the immigrant Five Civilized Tribes—the Choctaws, Chickasaws, Creeks, Seminoles, and Cherokees—owned the Indian Territory (today's Oklahoma minus the Panhandle and the extreme northeast corner) in fee simple through purchase from the federal government.[17]

However, the sale of these lands occurred without the knowledge or consent of Indian peoples already occupying them, and that fact created hard feelings and conflict that lasted a long time. The Wichitas believed they had reason to resent the coming of the southeastern nations. Although some Wichitas moved south into Texas

[15] Quoted in Foreman, "Survey of a Wagon Road," 76, 93.

[16] Gibson, *Oklahoma*, 42, 52.

[17] Gibson, *Oklahoma*, 41–83. The areas known as "Old Greer County," the southwest corner of Oklahoma, bounded by the North Fork of the Red River, was in dispute with the State of Texas until a Supreme Court ruling in 1896 declared it part of Oklahoma Territory.

Figure 17. Artist George Catlin drew a sketch of the U.S. Dragoons approaching a Comanche village in the Wichita Mountains in 1834. *Oklahoma Historical Society*

about 1811, others remained in present southwestern Oklahoma along Cache Creek near the Wichita Mountains. Their village in Devil's Canyon southeast of today's Quartz Mountain State Park was the destination for Col. Henry Dodge's Dragoon Expedition in 1834, the first official contact between the Plains tribes and the United States. Dodge invited them to meet with the immigrant tribes at Camp Holmes (near today's Lexington, Oklahoma) the following summer. In August 1835, 7,000 Indians met to discuss the new situation. All except the Kiowas signed the Camp Holmes Treaty, which pledged peaceful acceptance of each other's presence. At Fort Gibson in 1837, the Kiowas, Apaches, and Wichitas from Texas signed an almost identical treaty. These treaties did not refer to land claims or cessions, but they implied that the Plains tribes, who claimed territory and hunting rights as far east as the Cross Timbers, were yielding that claim by acknowledging the right of the immigrant tribes to occupy those lands. It was not long before the reality of conflicting claims diffused the mood of peace and good will. Years of complaints from the immigrant nations to Washington about depredations by the "wild tribes" on their western frontiers followed.[18]

[18] The Osages ceded their Indian Territory claims north of the Canadian River in 1825 and gradually moved north. The best discussion of this intertribal conflict is in David La Vere, *Contrary Neighbors: Southern Plains and Removed Indians in Indian Territory* (Norman: University of Oklahoma Press, 2000), 77–90.

Figure 18. These Caddos, shown participating in a Green Corn Dance, believed they had rights to the Washita River Valley.
Oklahoma Historical Society

The difficult position of the Wichitas exemplified the problem of conflicting claims. When interviewed in 2002, President Gary McAdams of the Wichita and Affiliated Tribes said, ". . . At some point, all the lands in Oklahoma that the Wichitas considered theirs since time immemorial were at various times given to different other tribes."[19] Including their traditional homelands in the Washita River Valley in the Choctaw and Chickasaw purchases ignored their historical association with these lands. They believed the Camp Holmes Treaty guaranteed their hunting rights in the vicinity of the Wichita Mountains.[20] In 1854 Toshaquash, second chief of the Wichitas, told federal officials through interpreter Jesse Chisholm that all the lands north of the Red River from the mouth of the Washita River to the 102d meridian had belonged to the Wichitas for four generations and that they had "never bartered or sold any portion of their country to the United States."[21] The next year, 1855, the federal government leased the western third of the Choctaw and Chickasaw country for the Wichitas. The "Leased District" included much of the traditional Wichita homeland in today's western Oklahoma, including the location of Washita Battlefield.[22]

Likewise, the Caddos—the Kadohadacho, Nachitoches, and Hasinai—believed that they had claims to the lands sold to the

[19] Interview of Gary McAdams, by Loretta Fowler, Anadarko, Oklahoma, November 8, 2002, in Fowler, *Draft Report, Phase III.*

[20] Fowler, *Final Report, Phase II*, 14–15.

[21] Quoted in La Vere, *Contrary Neighbors*, 142.

[22] Fowler, *Final Report, Phase II*, 15; Morris, Goins, and McReynolds, *Historical Atlas*, Map 26.

Figure 19. Chief Showetat, or Caddo George Washington, was a
leader of the Caddo tribe until 1883. *Oklahoma Historical Society*

Choctaws and Chickasaws. Earlier their homeland included the
lower Red River Valley in southeastern Oklahoma, but as game became scarce in the early 1800s they hunted as far west as the mouth
of the Washita River. Cecile Elkins Carter, a Caddo historian, offered proof of this in describing an incident recorded by John Sibley,
the first Caddo agent after the Louisiana Purchase. About 1807,
"Dayhoee, one of the very powerful, astute Caddo leaders . . . led this
hunting group all the way up to the Pani Pict, which of course were
the Wichita in what became Indian Territory. . . . They may very
well have been in the Washita River area. They would've been in the
Washita River area by 1807." The Caddos had gone to hunt bison
and raid for horses. It had been a successful trip because they were
coming home with more than twenty horses loaded with bison hides.
But, Carter continued,

> they were raided by a group of Osage, who were the bane of
> the Caddos from the time the French had contact with the
> Osage. . . . Beginning in the eighteenth century Osage raids on
> Caddo communities—particularly among the Kadohadacho
> —were very destructive. . . . They were miles still from home.
> So there they were, they were left without transportation . . . be-
> cause the Osage took all of the horses and, of course, took all of
> the hides. So Day-ho-ee had to send a runner back home to east
> Texas to say, "It's gonna be a while before we get home, folks."

So they gathered up as many horses as they could find in the villages and took them out and brought them back home. But we know from that, and we know that this was not a first trip, and it was not unusual for them to go that far. And certainly, like in the seventeenth century you had Caddo hunting west of Cross Timbers.[23]

As Anglo-American settlement encroached on their lands in Louisiana and Texas, Caddos moved back and forth across the Red River away from hostile and aggressive neighbors. The Whitebead band, however, remained near the lower Washita River in present Oklahoma. When the Leased District was created, the Caddos were promised land there between the Canadian and Red rivers between the 98th and 100th meridians. This, of course, also included the location of Washita Battlefield.[24]

During the late 1850s the Leased District served as a refuge for a number of tribes in addition to the Wichitas and Caddos. Continuing Texan hostility led finally to the evacuation of Indians from the reserves there. In 1859 Waco (Tawakoni Wichitas), Tonkawa, Anadarko, Ioni, Keechi, and Penateka Comanches moved into the Leased District, along with some Shawnees and Delawares. Wichita Agency was established on the Washita River west of present Anadarko to oversee these tribes and Fort Cobb was built to keep the peace.[25]

Keeping the peace had become a high priority as evidenced shortly before the tribes moved into the Leased District. Just the year before the Indians were expelled from Texas, Capt. John S. "Rip" Ford led 100 Texas Rangers on a punitive expedition against Comanches they suspected of depredations committed that spring. With them went 112 Reserve Indians—Caddo, Shawnee, Tonkawa, Anadarko, Delaware, Waco, and Kichai—led by Lawrence Sullivan "Sul" Ross. Crossing the Red River into the Indian Territory violated federal Indian law and the treaties with the immigrant nations. However, the Ranger-Indian force rode north across today's western Oklahoma and Roger Mills County following a travois trail toward the Antelope Hills. At dawn on May 12, 1858, they charged across the Canadian River and attacked a sleeping and relatively undefended Kotsoteka Comanche camp on Little Robe Creek. It lay at the west base of the Antelope Hills in present Ellis County, Oklahoma. While women and children scrambled into brushy ravines, Pohebits Quasho, or Iron Jacket, led the defense of the camp, which was overrun by noon. The Rangers and their Indian allies rounded up prisoners and 300 horses as they burned the camp. Indian accounts of the fight disputed Ford's claim that they had killed seventy-six Comanches, including women and children. Some historians argue that the Battle of Antelope Hills (or Little Robe Creek) es-

[23] Interview of Cecile Elkins Carter, by Loretta Fowler, Meade, Oklahoma, December 13, 2002, in Fowler, *Draft Report, Phase III.*

[24] Fowler, *Final Report, Phase II*, 48–52.

[25] Gibson, *The American Indian*, 347–348.

Figure 20. Apache Chief Tar Say, or Pacer, led his people as the Anglo-American frontier approached western Oklahoma. *Oklahoma Historical Society*

tablished that an Anglo-American military force could strike deep into Plains Indian country. Moreover, it set a precedent for launching punitive attacks on unsuspecting Indian camps without regard for the guilt or identity of the inhabitants. At any rate, there was a marked similarity between this attack and the Washita Massacre ten years later at Washita Battlefield. Likewise, just a few months after the Ranger-Indian attack, a cavalry column commanded by Maj. Earl Van Dorn struck Comanche and Wichita camps near present Rush Springs, Oklahoma.[26]

It is clear that the area around today's Washita Battlefield was attractive in the first half of the 1800s. It was common ground on the frontier between the Comanches, Kiowas, and Apaches who ranged to the south and the Cheyennes and Arapahos who generally stayed farther north. It was a place to socialize and trade for these five tribes that had put their differences behind them. The sheltered upper Washita River Valley was a good location for a camp, winter or summer. In addition to the bison on which so much of Plains culture and livelihood depended, there were many other game animals, birds, and fish they used for food, shelter, furnishings, clothing, games, decoration, and ceremonies. There were plants—berries, nuts, bulbs, seeds, leaves, stalks, saps, and fruits— women used for food, healing,

[26] La Vere, *Contrary Neighbors*, 154–155; Joseph Thoburn, "A Campaign of the Texas Rangers Against Comanches," *Sturm's Oklahoma Magazine* 10 (July 1910):30–38; Walter Prescott Webb, *The Texas Rangers: A Century of Frontier Defense* (Boston: Houghton Mifflin Company, 1935), 151–158; Rupert Norval Richardson, *The Comanche Barrier to South Plains Settlement: A Century and a Half of Savage Resistance to the Advancing White Frontier* (Glendale, Calif.: Arthur H. Clark, 1933), 236–237; Stan Hoig, *Tribal Wars of the Southern Plains* (Norman: University of Oklahoma Press, 1993), 160–166; Gibson, *Oklahoma*, 115.

tools, containers, dyes, fuels, and windbreaks. Along the riverbanks were cottonwoods, willows, elms, dogwoods, hackberries, oaks, and cedars for fuel, arrow shafts, baskets, fish and bird traps, rope, stirrups, drumsticks, glues, lodge poles, and ceremonial items. There was stone to straighten arrows and shape into axe heads. There were sunflowers for yellow dye and red shale to be ground up for red paint. There was adequate water, and there were grass and cottonwood bark to feed the horse herds.[27]

Alonzo Chalepah, of today's Apache Tribe of Oklahoma, remembered that his ancestors found the upper Washita River Valley a very good place to camp. There were "nuts such as pecans and walnuts, later on would come persimmons. Roots wouldn't be too much and berries wouldn't be around in the winter season. However, in summer we would have a variety of plums, prickly pear, and those kinds of things we could gather. Those are some of the things that we highly relied on to gather and to eat, because nowadays we know that they're highly nutritious. And the game was not real rare at that time...."[28] Indeed, the game was plentiful, especially bison, and the river was full of catfish and turtles. "You could get anything you wanted," along the Washita River, according to Moses Starr, a Cheyenne who grew up on its banks a century later.[29] Anglo-Americans also saw potential in the area for farmers and livestock raisers, and for travelers by road or rail across the Southern Plains by way of the Washita-Canadian river divide. But federal policy had removed the area from possible non-Indian settlement by creating the "Indian Territory" as a new homeland for removed tribes. Unfortunately, in doing so the government had generated a sense of betrayal not only among the removed tribes, but also among those who had regarded the lands as their traditional homelands.

[27] Fowler, *Final Report, Phase II*, 17–20.

[28] Interview of Alonzo Chalepah, by Loretta Fowler, Apache, Oklahoma, March 31, 2003, in Fowler, *Draft Report, Phase III*.

[29] Fowler, *Final Report, Phase II*, 44.

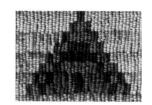

Chapter 4

TO SLEEP IN PEACE

Although the Civil War is generally thought of as an event that happened in the East, it had a long-term impact on the Indian Territory. It set off major changes for Indian people, especially for those on the Southern Plains. The impact on the Cheyennes was particularly bitter.

The Civil War temporarily halted the removal of tribes to the Indian Territory from 1862 to 1865. Intertribal and intratribal violence and chaos devastated eastern Indian Territory, scattered its 100,000 inhabitants, impoverished them, and greatly reduced their number. However, sparsely inhabited western Indian Territory was relatively untouched. The great impact of the war on that part of the territory occurred in 1866. That year the federal government imposed punishing Reconstruction treaties on the Cherokee, Choctaw, Chickasaw, Creek, and Seminole nations because each had signed treaties of alliance with the Confederacy in 1861. The Cherokees ceded their Outlet; the Creeks ceded the western half of their domain; the Seminoles lost all their lands; and the Choctaws and Chickasaws ceded the Leased District for $300,000. Federal plans were to settle additional tribes yet to be removed on reservations on the ceded lands.[1]

The process had already started when the Reconstruction treaties were signed. Federal officials met with the Plains tribes on the Little Arkansas River in 1865. The Kiowas and Comanches accepted a large reservation bounded by the Cimarron and Red rivers between the 98th and the 103d meridians. This included the location of the Washita Battlefield National Historic Site. The Cheyennes, Arapahos, and Apaches were to confederate on a reservation between the Arkansas and Cimarron rivers in Kansas and northern Indian Territory, after giving up all lands north of the Arkansas River. Within two years, though, Anglo-American settlement, stimulated by the end of the Civil War, pressed into the newly created reservations, requiring reduced acreage and new treaties. The Medicine Lodge Council in 1867 redrew the reservation boundaries. According to the Medicine Lodge Treaty, the Kiowas, Comanches, and Apaches were assigned to the old Leased District south of the Washita River. The

[1] Gibson, *Oklahoma*, 117–129.

Figure 21. The Cheyennes, Arapahos, Kiowas, Apaches, and Comanches agreed to reservations in western Oklahoma at the Medicine Lodge Council in 1867. *Taken from Harper's Weekly, November 16, 1867.*

Cheyennes and Arapahos were assigned lands between the Cimarron and Arkansas rivers in the Cherokee Outlet. Their objections to the new location led in 1869 to a third and final reservation south of the Cherokee Outlet, north of the Kiowa-Comanche-Apache Reservation, and between the 98th and 100th meridians. In 1872 the federal government reduced the Cheyenne and Arapaho Reservation some 600,000 acres by carving out the Wichita-Caddo Reservation for those tribes, the Absentee Delawares, Keechis, Anadarkos, and Wacos.[2]

Getting the Plains tribes to move onto the reservations, give up their nomadic ways, and accept Anglo-American culture set up as the ideal proved very difficult and resulted in warfare on the Southern Plains from 1868 to 1875. Among the tribes most deeply involved were the Cheyennes. Although they had been signatories at the Medicine Lodge Council, not all agreed with the provisions of the treaty. Cheyenne culture and organization was strongly associated with the message of Sweet Medicine, formulated about the end of the eighteenth century when they were living near the Black Hills and Bear Butte. While the Council of Forty-four chiefs, including the four peace chiefs, led the tribe, warrior societies such as the Dog Men were a powerful influence. The latter objected to giving up their hunting grounds in Kansas and confinement to the Indian Territory reservation. Recent history also affected Cheyenne views of Anglo-Americans. They remembered the 1864 surprise attack of Colorado militia, led by Col. John Chivington, on the camp of Peace

[2] Ibid., 143–146.

Chief Black Kettle at Sand Creek, Colorado Territory. The memory fed Cheyenne distrust of the Anglo-American "spiders."[3]

Continuing violence associated with Plains Indian resistance to confinement on the new reservations led in 1868 to a military campaign into the Indian Territory. Brig. Gen. Alfred Sully led an ineffective expedition from Kansas against the Cheyennes in early fall 1868. Nine companies of the Seventh Cavalry, three of the Third Infantry, and their supply wagons bogged down in the sand hills near the junction of Wolf and Beaver creeks near present Woodward, Oklahoma. The expedition turned back after the Second Battle of Wolf Creek, more farce than battle, took place on October 13. The expedition had proved that a large, slow-moving invasion was ineffective against mobile, skilled guerrilla fighters such as the Plains tribes. The situation called for new tactics.[4]

The new approach was winter war. Gen. Philip Sheridan ordered strikes against the Plains tribes during the season they felt most secure in their camps. A three-pronged offensive began later that fall, with columns setting out from Fort Dodge, Kansas, Fort Lyon, Colorado, and Fort Bascom, New Mexico. Their orders were to attack wherever they found the Indians, destroy their shelters and supplies, kill the men, capture the women and children, and destroy the horse herds. This would end the Indians' mobility and force them onto the reservations to avoid exposure and starvation. The column from Fort Lyon completed its patrol without intercepting any Indians. Lt. Col. George Armstrong Custer, commanding the Seventh Cavalry in the Fort Dodge column, moved south from newly established Camp Supply at the junction of Wolf and Beaver creeks. Guided by Osage scouts, they followed a trail toward the Washita River and discovered the camp of Cheyenne Peace Chief Black Kettle. At dawn on November 27 their charge into the sleeping camp initiated the Washita Massacre. While the "Battle of the Washita" was well-publicized as a Custer victory, a similar attack during the same operation received little attention. The Fort Bascom column, 200 cavalry and infantry commanded by Maj. A. W. Evans, followed a trail across the Texas Panhandle toward Devil's Canyon on the North Fork of the Red River. On Christmas Day at Soldier Spring near the intersection of the Greer, Kiowa, and Jackson county lines today, they attacked a Nokoni Comanche camp on the riverbank. Here, too, the cavalry burned tepees and provisions and fouled the water in the spring by throwing in ten tons of dried buffalo meat. The Comanches later renamed the spring "dried-beef pond." As was the case at the fight on the Washita River, the cavalry came under counterattack from Comanches and Kiowas camped downstream. After the troops withdrew, the Comanches either went to Fort Cobb for refuge or joined the Quahadi Comanches on the Staked Plains.[5]

[3] Fowler, *Final Report, Phase II*, 11–12, 20–21, 23–24.

[4] Hoig, *Tribal Wars*, 233, 244–248, 252–253; Leckie, *Military Conquest*, 81–83; Louise Boyd James, *Below Devil's Gap: The Story of Woodward County* (Perkins, Okla.: Evans Publications, 1984), 1–3.

[5] Leckie, *Military Conquest*, 114–118; Nye, *Carbine and Lance*, 100–107.

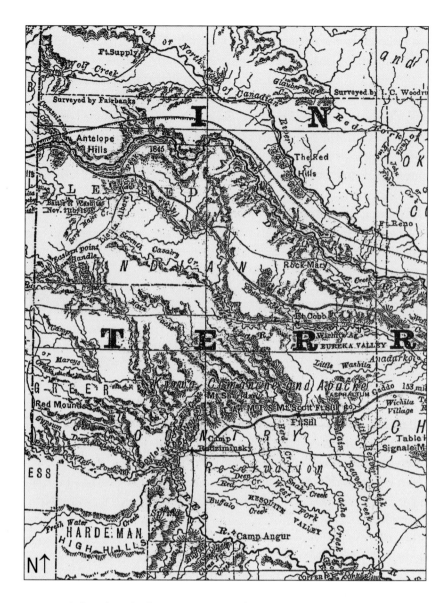

Map 5. This detail of an 1889 map shows the military posts established in western Oklahoma during the Plains Wars.[6]

Through the winter and early spring of 1869, the effort continued to bring in the Cheyennes. In mid-March Custer located them along the Sweetwater River in the Texas Panhandle and sat down to negotiate their surrender and the return of white captives. During a parlay with Medicine Arrows, the chief smoked with Custer and then emptied the pipe ashes over his boots with a warning not to attack the Cheyennes again. To Cheyennes, this signified that Custer must keep faith with them or be blown away like the ashes. This event, which apparently had little meaning for Custer, became part of Cheyenne understanding of their history during those troubled times and into the next century.[7] In 2000 Eugene Blackbear, Sr., stated, "Custer had it coming, what happened to him. But he was

[6] Detail of "Indian Territory, 1889," 2000.208, Oklahoma Historical Society, Oklahoma City, Oklahoma.

[7] Berthrong, *The Southern Cheyennes*, 336–337.

warned. He was told not never attack Cheyennes anymore, but he didn't listen."[8]

According to Alonzo Chalepah, the Washita Massacre marked a turning point for his tribe, the Apaches, and the other Plains Tribes. "At that time of history we've seen that the knowledge of the population of the white man was unknown," he said. From "feeling confident and united with other tribes as allies," doubt entered their consideration of the future. Customarily,

> tribes came together and met and discussed, not war . . . not an aggressive war, but a defense war, perhaps, because we were beginning to find out at that time that a place called Washington and in between here and there were more people than leaves in the forest they used to say, or stars in the sky. What's happening at that time was to seek other directions as to how to live with the white man because we knew they were coming and coming in more numbers, and that their military was, more or less from what we'd seen, was the aggressor. . . . Our concern was afterwards . . . how did the military find out who was Cheyenne and who was a Kiowa and who was an Apache?[9]

The Apaches had not seen the massacre, but they heard it in the distance and heard from other tribes what had happened there. Chalepah continued, "So the Cheyenne who suffered that, we expected that to happen to us, too." The tribes scattered, looking for refuge, perhaps following the Kiowas and Comanches to Palo Duro Canyon in the Texas Panhandle. The Apaches felt "a big concern because it was a campaign of military against children and elders, and that's why we had to be on the ready."[10]

Although the military eventually forced the Southern Plains tribes onto their designated reservations, there were six more years of sporadic resistance and experimentation with suppressing it, even though some tribes developed peace factions or chose not to resist. The last major incident was the Outbreak of 1874 (Red River War, Buffalo War), in which at least a part of the Cheyennes, Arapahos, Kiowas, and Comanches fought as allies. Indian frustration erupted over the inroads of commercial bison hunters into the Southern Plains herds, horse theft by non-Indians, and attempts to stop Indian raiding outside their reservations. War parties, sometimes including members of several tribes, attacked hunters at Adobe Walls and travelers on the roads into neighboring states. The war ended with the Battle of Palo Duro Canyon, which forced hostile Plains Indians out of their stronghold in the Texas Panhandle.[11]

Warfare for the Cheyennes did not completely end, even though the military generally succeeded in suppressing resistance of the Southern Plains tribes by 1875. The Cheyenne tribe had gradually split into northern and southern divisions about the middle of

[8] Interview of Eugene Blackbear, Sr., by Loretta Fowler, Norman, Oklahoma, September 20, 2000, in Fowler, *Final Report, Phase II*, 84.

[9] Interview of Alonzo Chalepah, March 31, 2003, in Fowler, Draft *Report, Phase III*.

[10] Ibid.

[11] Gibson, *The American Indian*, 412.

Figure 22. Gen. Philip Sheridan ordered the winter campaigns against the Plains Indians to force them onto reservations. *Oklahoma Historical Society*

the century. Even so, there was frequent interaction between the bands on the Southern Plains and the Northern Plains. Northern Cheyennes continued their warfare with the United States, participating in the massacre of Custer and the Seventh Cavalry at the Little Bighorn in 1876. For Cheyennes, this was both retribution and a fulfillment of Medicine Arrow's prophecy. Several Washita survivors, such as Magpie, participated in the battle. Once United States warfare with the Northern Plains tribes ended in 1877, the Northern Cheyennes were sent to join their kinsmen on the Cheyenne and Arapaho Reservation. Never content there and suffering illnesses in the alien environment, some attempted to return to the north in September 1878 under the leadership of Dull Knife (Morning Star) and Lone Wolf. They left a trail of death and destruction across western Kansas before being recaptured in Nebraska and assigned to a northern reservation.[12]

For Southern Cheyennes, especially, along with their neighbors, it was difficult to put the past away, even when they were settled on the Cheyenne and Arapaho Reservation. In 1899 Ben Clark, looking back at the Washita Massacre, was quoted as saying, "There are still Indians in western Oklahoma who bear scars received on that cold November day." A reporter wrote, "Chief Red Moon and his untamable band of Cheyennes whose camp is on the Washita, about

[12] Brill, "End of the Cheyenne Trail"; Donald J. Berthrong, *The Cheyenne and Arapaho Ordeal: Reservation and Agency Life in the Indian Territory, 1875–1907* (Norman: University of Oklahoma Press, 1976), 32–37.

46

Figure 23. Chief Little Raven led Arapahos in defending Black Kettle's camp. *Oklahoma Historical Society*

twenty miles above [the town of] Cheyenne, still nurse the hatreds and heartaches caused by the slaughter."[13]

For the Washita generation, being able to take their moccasins off before going to sleep was still a luxury. There was no longer a need to sleep in one's moccasins to be prepared for a surprise attack. A century later in 1999, Kathryn Bull Coming (born 1913) recalled childhood bedtime stories from her grandparents about their Washita memories: "One night when we was all going to bed, we had no televisions, nothing to do, just go to bed and go to sleep. We asked my grandpa. . . . He said, 'You're all right tonight. You take your shoes off, you get up any time you want to . . . In our days over here,' he said, 'white people was fighting us, soldiers." Her grandmother told how Black Kettle's people said, when warned about the approach of possible enemies, "'No. We just had peace treaty.'" Told that soldiers were coming, some Cheyennes said "'Oh, you don't have to run again . . . We got flag.'" But her grandmother's frightened parents sent her away with the warning, "'Keep goin'. Don't stop. We're goin' all get killed over here. . . .' That was the last I hear from my mother and my dad.'" When the attack came, "My grandma was telling me, was way off already, and then she knew she didn't have no folks, no home." Two generations later Kathryn Bull Coming's grandmother tucked her grandchildren in with the words, "'They

[13] "Custer's Washita Fight."

47

Figure 24. No longer able to hunt bison, Cheyennes and Arapahos gathered to receive rations from their agents. *Oklahoma Historical Society*

don't do that any more now,' she said, 'You're all right, you sleep good at night. In our days we don't sleep good.'"[14]

The original philosophy for reserving land for Indians had some benign elements. A reservation, humanitarians believed, would shelter them from contact with the worst elements of non-Indian society and prevent conflict with non-Indians, thus saving Indian lives in the long run. Non-Indians without official permission would be kept outside the boundaries, while teachers and missionaries eradicated Indian cultures, educated them in Anglo-American ways, and prepared Indian people for eventual American citizenship. At the same time, though, confining Indians to reservations served the practical purpose of freeing up land non-Indian farmers could develop in safety and use better, they believed, than nomadic hunters.[15]

However, the isolation intended in this rationale never really existed on most Indian reservations, including the Cheyenne and Arapaho Reservation. The Plains Wars of 1867–1875 and continuing Indian restlessness compelled the United States Army to make Camp (then Fort) Supply permanent. New posts at Fort Sill in the Kiowa-Comanche-Apache Reservation, at Fort Reno on the eastern edge of the Cheyenne and Arapaho lands, and at Cantonment midway between Reno and Supply were also established (See Map 5). White troops along with the African-American "buffalo soldiers" of the Ninth and Tenth Cavalry and the Twenty-fourth Infantry garrisoned these posts. They were there to suppress Indian rebellion and keep "intruders" out of the reservations—horse thieves, timber thieves, hunters, cattlemen, and would-be settlers. However, there

[14] Interview of Kathryn Bull Coming, by Mary Jane Warde, Seiling, Oklahoma vicinity, March 26, 1999, in Warde, *Final Report, Phase I.*

[15] Berthrong, *Cheyenne and Arapaho Ordeal*, 416.

Figure 25. Cattlemen used the grasslands of the Cheyenne and Arapaho Reservation to graze their herds. *Oklahoma Historical Society*

were many non-Indians legitimately in the Cheyenne and Arapaho Reservation: agency staff, boarding school staff, military contractors, and the missionaries—among them Quakers, Mennonites, Amish, Methodists, and Episcopalians—who came to convert the Indians to Christianity. Roads and two primary north-south cattle trails developed through the reservation as the range cattle industry flourished in the late 1860s. The Chisholm Trail passed through or near the eastern boundary, and the Great Western Cattle Trail connected Texas and Kansas, crossing the reservation near present Sentinel, Canute, Hammon, and Leedy, Oklahoma. Cattlemen initially allowed into the reservation to supply beef to the army and hungry Indians lingered to graze their herds on reservation grass. As cattlemen moved into the Texas Panhandle after the Plains Wars ended, they also allowed their herds to stray onto Indian land. Corporate ranching came to the reservation in 1883. The Cheyenne and Arapaho Stock Growers Association eventually leased 4 million acres of the reservation before Pres. Grover Cleveland ordered them out in 1885.[16]

Reservation life was a difficult adjustment for all the Southern Plains tribes confined on the Indian Territory reservations. In the 1870s commercial hide hunters annihilated the bison herds so vital to their subsistence and cultures, and they had not yet acquired the

[16] Charles L. Kenner, *Buffalo Soldiers & Officers of the Ninth Cavalry, 1867–1898: Black & White Together* (Norman: University of Oklahoma Press, 1999), 152; Arlen LeRoy Fowler, *The Black Infantry in the West, 1869–1891* (Norman: University of Oklahoma Press, 1971, paperback edition, 1996), 74–77; H. S. Tennant, "The Two Cattle Trails," *The Chronicles of Oklahoma* 14 (March 1936):84–122. For cattle ranching see Edward Everett Dale, *Ranching on the Cheyenne- Arapaho Reservation, 1880–1885*, Oklahoma Historical Society, Oklahoma City, Oklahoma.

information, skills, tools, and resources to be farmers and ranchers, roles thrust on them by federal Indian agents. They were dependent on beef and flour rations distributed by the agent, but periodic reductions made the situation worse. Cheyennes and Arapahos hunted whatever small game was available, fished, and gathered edible plants. Restricted to their own reservation limits, they were sometimes cut off from places that had spiritual meaning and from plants and other resources that had spiritual, cultural, or medicinal uses.[17]

Federal officials also began a program to educate Indian children, preferably by removing them from tribal and family settings. Over the next few years day and boarding schools for Cheyenne and Arapaho children opened at Concho near Darlington Agency, Cantonment, Whirlwind, Seger Colony, and Red Moon, the last just east of today's Hammon, Oklahoma. Others were sent to Chilocco in northern Indian Territory or to Carlisle Indian School in Pennsylvania. The curriculum of all these schools was vocational, and school staff forced students to speak English instead of their own languages. Carlisle grew out of the imprisonment at Fort Marion, St. Augustine, Florida, in 1875 of the "worst" Indian offenders in the recent wars. Some such as Making Medicine, who took the name David Pendleton Oakerhater, became literate and were converted to Christianity. Many returned convinced that Indians had no choice but to follow the white man's road.[18]

In spite of the presence of the military—and partly because of it—Cheyennes and Arapahos lived in fear of the white man. Intruders in their reservation victimized them by stealing their stock, timber, and other resources, but federal officials failed to uphold their property rights. Although the agents tried to disperse them throughout the reservation, they preferred to live in bands for safety as they had before confinement to the reservation. Some survivors of the Washita Massacre lived with Red Moon's band. They settled in the Washita River Valley upstream from today's Washita Battlefield National Historic Site and lived somewhat better by collecting tolls in the form of cattle from herds that trespassed on their land from the Texas Panhandle. Other survivors and their descendants could later be found among Cheyenne communities at Watonga, Seiling, Clinton, and El Reno.[19]

Major change occurred again with the passage of the Dawes (General Allotment) Act in 1887. This policy required Indians to become individual landowners, a difficult departure for cultures that did not conceive of land as something that could be owned. Rather, it was similar to air and water in that it was free to all. The resources of territory claimed by a tribe were shared within the community. The Dawes Act provided for the division of reservations into allotments, generally 160 acres each. These were to be assigned to indi-

[17] Fowler, *Final Report, Phase II*, 36–37.

[18] The best source is Berthrong, *Cheyenne and Arapaho Ordeal*. Nye, *Carbine and Lance*, 231.

[19] Interview of Rollin Haag, by Loretta Fowler, Calumet, Oklahoma, December 18, 2000, in Fowler, *Final Report, Phase II*, 37–38.

Figure 26. Cheyenne boys and girls wore military-style uniforms at Cantonment Indian School. *Western History Collections, University of Oklahoma Libraries*

vidual Indians in the hope of undermining tribalism, transforming them into farmers, and preparing them for American citizenship. At the same time, "surplus" lands remaining once each tribal member received his or her allotment could be opened to non-Indian home-steaders for settlement. Eugene Blackbear, Sr., summarized, ". . . Each time we were given land the white people settlers have always liked our land and they always cried around to the government, 'We want that land.' And then the government has to maneuver us around and talk us out of it, or cheat us out of it. Then their white settlers . . . come in and settle on it. It happened to us lotta times."[20] Very few Indians wanted the changes allotment would bring, but, powered by the federal government, reformers, commercial interests, railroads, and would-be settlers, it occurred over their objections.[21]

While the negotiations prior to allotment took place, Chey-ennes and Arapahos, along with members of several other tribes in the Indian Territory, looked for relief from these troubled times. In 1890 news came that Wovoka, a Paiute, was urging Indians to return to the old ways to bring back the bison and drive out the white man. The Ghost Dance phenomenon attracted many followers in the territory, which was a great concern to agents, teachers, and neighbors on the reservations. However, no serious outburst oc-curred in the Indian Territory, and the "craze" soon passed away.[22]

The allotment process assigned most Cheyennes and Arapa-hos individual holdings on the North Canadian River through the

[20] Interview of Eugene Blackbear, Sr., by Loretta Fowler, Norman, Oklahoma, September 20, 2000, in ibid., 82.

[21] See Berthrong, *Cheyenne and Arapaho Ordeal*, 148–181.

[22] Ibid., 138–139.

reservation; on the Canadian River generally downstream from Thomas, Oklahoma; and along the Washita River from the big bend east of Cheyenne through today's Hammon and Clinton, Oklahoma. There were no allotments very near Washita Battlefield National Historic Site. The closest substantial area of Cheyenne settlement was along White Shield Creek, a tributary of the Washita River just west of today's Hammon, Oklahoma, named for the chief who eventually replaced Red Moon as leader of that band.[23] Moses Starr noted, "All along that Washita River there was a lot of Indians. You know, during the time that they gave them allotments, water was really important to the Indians, so all the Indians chose along the Washita River. That's where they lived because they wanted to live by the river where water was available, and the trees and the game were."[24] Some, such as the Red Moon band, resisted taking the white man's road. They preferred to live together along White Shield Creek rather than spread out to their allotments, to live in tepees rather than houses, and to keep their children at home rather than send them away to school.[25]

As the end of the nineteenth century neared, the Washita generation of Cheyennes, along with their Plains Indian neighbors, looked back on changes that rocked the foundations of their cultures—the coming of large numbers of Anglo-Americans, removal from territory and resources basic to their way of life, warfare, and dispossession. Yet they were, and are, survivors, and they found ways to go on.

[23] Ibid., 213, 230, 249.

[24] Interview of Moses Starr, by Loretta Fowler, Weatherford, Oklahoma, March 26, 2001, in Fowler, *Final Report, Phase II*, 160.

[25] Berthrong, *Cheyenne and Arapaho Ordeal*, 213, 230, 249.

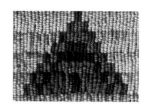

Chapter 5

COMING OUT ON TOP

The opening of the Cheyenne and Arapaho Reservation allowed the first large influx of non-Indian settlers into the vicinity of Washita Battlefield National Historic Site. The entry method selected, the land run, was the third of five in Oklahoma history. At the signal, the potential homesteader would race to a location he or she favored, drive in stakes to mark a 160–acre claim, and then file the proper paperwork at the designated federal land office. At the appointed time on April 19, 1892—and times varied by county—the run for land in the Cheyenne and Arapaho Reservation would begin, an hour or two earlier than the run for lots in designated town sites. To reduce the number of "sooners" (those who attempted to enter early) and prevent the engrossment of land by speculators, the announcement of the opening was publicized only one week ahead, effectively limiting land run participation to legitimate homesteaders, generally residents of nearby Texas, Kansas, and Oklahoma Territory. To make the survey markers visible, the prairie grasses were burned off.[1]

People lined up along the borders of the reservation hoped to recreate the life they had left behind while improving their fortunes. Most people who are content with their present circumstances do not pull up stakes and set off toward an unknown land and an uncertain future. But those times were difficult for people whose livelihood came from the soil. The range cattle industry that had boomed in the 1870s was in severe decline by 1890. Great Plains farmers in the 1880s faced a cycle of drought and severe winters along with high prices for farm machinery, crop storage, and shipping. Many were in debt while crop prices were low, money tight, and credit scarce. The South, too, was still impoverished in the aftermath of the Civil War. For some, the lands being opened in the Cheyenne and Arapaho Reservation, along with the other Indian Territory reservations, offered opportunities for a fresh start on a 160–acre homestead with five years to make improvements—"prove up"—and pay the federal government the going rate, generally about $1.25 per acre.

But it is estimated that only 25,000 to 30,000 potential homesteaders made the run into the Cheyenne and Arapaho Reservation. There was a widely held belief that these western prairies were too

[1] A good account of the opening of the Cheyenne and Arapaho Reservation is Michael H. Reggio, "Troubled Times: Homesteading in Short-Grass Country, 1892–1900," *The Chronicles of Oklahoma* 57 (Summer 1979):196–211.

Figure 27. The Parnell family on their Dewey County homestead in 1908. *Oklahoma Historical Society*

dry for farming and that the land was good only for cattle grazing. Fear of the Cheyennes and Arapahos also kept some away. Nor were there railroads or roads for ready access to market for the farmer's crops. So three months after the opening in April 1892, Oklahoma Territorial Gov. Abraham J. Seay estimated that 2.8 million acres, approximately 80 percent, of lands available in the former reservation lay unclaimed. In the 20 percent claimed, mostly in the eastern areas, the non-Indian population stood at 7,600. The April opening date made it too late in the growing season to break the tough sod and plant crops. Moreover, the region was from 1885 to 1896 in the grip of severe drought. Many of those who made the run did not stay, and available claims filled in slowly over the next decade.[2]

Although some homesteaders arrived with adequate resources, many came with very little of the equipment or capital needed to improve a claim. The fortunate brought milk cows, horses, oxen, chickens, groceries, and fabric for new clothing, along with furniture and the occasional musical instrument. Mrs. W. P. Hickman came from Missouri in 1899 with her mother, husband, and children to claims near Berlin in southern Roger Mills County. They shipped their belongings by rail to Weatherford, paying eighty dollars for a freight car and forty dollars for a livestock car for their three cows, three horses, and dozen chickens. The Stubbs family arrived in a horse-

[2] Ibid., 196–199.

drawn covered wagon with a herd of milk cows they had purchased on the way. Anna L. Green recalled that in November 1900 she and her husband, her parents, a brother and his family, and a friend moved from Nebraska to the claims they had staked earlier in what was then Roger Mills County, now Beckham County. The group traveled in four covered wagons and a buggy. Her brother arrived ill and with thirty cents in his pocket. M. W. Slatten came to Washita County from Georgia with his wife and five children. Slatten recalled that they had no place to stay after he arrived, and he did not have a dollar in his pocket. He built a dugout on his brother's place and tried to farm. But four dry years brought no profit, and the family moved on to Texas before eventually returning to Oklahoma.[3]

Excitement and expectation sometimes turned to dismay as soon as homesteaders reached their new land. Anna L. Green remembered that they were so excited to be nearing their claims that for the first time in their thirty-eight-day journey they broke their rule against Sunday travel. However, they discovered that the land covered in waving green grass in the summer looked far less inviting in December. "All we could see," she recalled, "was red hills and rock." The men went out to explore and came back "the sickest bunch I ever saw." Anna's father wanted to go back to Nebraska right then, but her mother refused, saying, "since she had come she was going to stay and . . . she had not wanted to come in the first place." Anna was equally determined. "My husband wanted to go back but I said we were not going back, for the last thing I had seen and heard was a bunch of people waving and saying, 'You all will be back.'"[4]

The first necessity after arriving was to provide shelter. Homesteaders made tents and wagon boxes serve—sometimes for months or years—until they could create more substantial housing. Anna Green's family lived in a tent, giving priority to building a barn of cottonwood logs for the livestock. But the wind battered the tent so much they hung a carpet to divide the barn and moved in with the animals. The green cottonwood lumber soon shrank, causing the barn to leak badly. Anna gave birth to a son with her bed covered by a wagon sheet thrown over the rafters to keep off the rain.[5]

Dugouts provided cheap and simple shelter, given the lack of building materials available, and they were usually the homesteader's first choice. They could be very basic. The six members of the T. F. Skelton family lived in "a hole down in the ground . . . covered over with dirt, a hole being left to get in and out."[6] Dugouts could also be more elaborate. H. W. Slatten recalled:

> Our dugout we lived in for four years was dug into the ground and covered with big logs through the center, willow brush on top of the logs, then hay, and then that was covered with dirt. A

[3] Interviews of Mrs. W. P. Hickman, 92: 457; James Allen Stubbs, 87:436; Anna L. Green, 84:361; M. W. Slatten, 101:469, Indian-Pioneer History, Oklahoma Historical Society, Oklahoma City, Oklahoma (hereafter cited as IPH).

[4] Interview of Anna L. Green, 84:362, IPH.

[5] Ibid., 366.

[6] Interview of T. F. Skelton, 101:437, IPH.

stovepipe ran out the top of the ground. Our furniture consisted of a little cook stove, bedsteads and chairs which I made from cottonwood poles, also a table made from boxes the Arbuckle coffee came in, and I made a safe to put the dishes in. I fixed a fireplace in the dugout and made the chimney out of sod. We had bed ticks filled with the prairie hay we gathered and at nights we would lay the bed ticks on the ground and all who could get on the bedstead would and the rest of us would pile on the ground.[7]

Half-dugouts were a variation. Julie Ann Morgan and her husband filed on a claim in southeastern Roger Mills County. Mrs. Morgan described the home her husband built using cottonwood logs from their claim:

He then made a half-dugout, size 12 x 12, dug down in the ground about three feet then walled it on up with lumber and covered it with logs and dirt and made a dirt fireplace in the back. Our dugout had a dirt floor and no windows. I did my cooking on the fireplace when I didn't cook on a fire outside. Our bedsteads were made of cottonwood poles with planks nailed across for slats and our mattress was a tick filled with prairie hay and my dresser was made from boxes. . . . There was a baby born to us after we filed on our claim and that made ten of us who lived in our dugout and tent.[8]

According to Annie Timmons, half-dugouts were the housing choice in southwestern Washita County. She and her family lived in a tent until they could bring lumber from El Reno to build a two-room box house, but they used a half-dugout for cooking. All together, twenty-four relatives and friends shared the Timmons home their first winter, 1897. In 2002 Clara King Davis described the half-dugout her family shared for several years in mid-twentieth-century Roger Mills County. It was very comfortable—warm in the winter and cool in the summer—but insects and snakes also found it inviting.[9]

Homesteaders found scarcities in their new western Oklahoma lands. Lucky settlers had a spring or good water in a creek. Unlucky pioneers hauled water from elsewhere or dug wells. Buffalo chips substituted for wood as fuel, but lumber for buildings and fences was expensive and harder to come by. Settlers sometimes solved that problem by cutting timber where they could find it—in the Canadian River breaks, in canyons that had not been homesteaded, and on Indian allotments. B. F. Pyle, who homesteaded in Roger Mills County near the old Herring Ranch, declared himself innocent when his Cheyenne neighbor Old Heap Crow suspected him of stealing timber from his allotment. However, Pyle often traded with the Indians for wood and had earlier turned a profit of $170 from a

[7] Interview of H. W. Slatten, 101:471, IPH.

[8] Interview of Julie Ann Morgan, 81: 104–105, IPH.

[9] Interview of Annie I. Timmons, 112: 245–246, IPH; interview of Clara King Davis and Lester R. Davis, by Mary Jane Warde, Cheyenne, Oklahoma, vicinity, October 16, 2002, in Mary Jane Warde, *Draft Report, Ethnographic Overview and Assessment of the Relationship between Washita Battlefield National Historic Site and the Traditional Associations of the Local Non-Indian communities and Landowners (Phase IV)*, Cooperative Agreement No. 1443CA125098002 (Modification 6), National Park Service, April 2, 2003.

winter spent cutting and hauling cedar poles from the Canadian River Valley. In fact, in the mid–1890s, before federal officials stepped in, settlers were stripping Indian allotments of walnut, hickory, and cedar logs, which they shipped out of El Reno by the carload. Annie Timmons remembered that men also risked arrest and detention at Anadarko when they slipped into the Kiowa-Comanche-Apache Reservation to cut wood.[10]

In fact, most homesteaders earned so little income from their new lands in the first years after the opening that they took whatever work they could find—and there was not much. Often they left their claims to find employment elsewhere, going as far as Kansas and Texas and returning when they had enough cash to keep going for a while longer. H. W. Slatten laid ties for the St. Louis and San Francisco Railroad to support his family. He remembered, "I would walk seven miles to work on the railroad and work from sunup to sundown for one dollar a day. I worked through all kinds of weather. It didn't make any difference, anyway to make a living for my family." Unfortunately, there was sometimes not enough food for all seven Slattens.[11] Henry Green worked as a freighter out of Weatherford, while his wife Anna looked after the family and farmed their land. James Allen Stubbs remembered a Washita County neighbor who had a large family, good people but poor. Every day the boys rode ten miles into Cloud Chief to pick up bundles of clothing, which their mothers and sisters would launder and the boys would return cleaned. The money the family earned fed them and allowed them to hold onto their claim. Stubbs and his family fed themselves by cutting wood and building dugouts for Kiowa Indians on the neighboring reservation. They also hauled stone for the construction of Rainy Mountain School and traded with the Kiowa Indians, exchanging corn and watermelons for the Kiowas' government-issued, whiteman clothing. All of the Stubbs's enterprises on the Kiowa lands were illegal.[12]

Women often contributed more than their share of the effort needed to create their new homes. In addition to childcare and homemaking, they helped with the heavy work of farming and sometimes took primary responsibility for the family and its claim. When the Green family planted their first crop, Anna dropped the seed in the furrows while her husband covered it with a sod plow. Mrs. U. T. Shanley drilled a well with a hand-turned augur in exchange for a pig.[13] Annie Timmons and her sons plowed the first sod for their crops on their Washita County homestead because her husband was sick that year. She recalled, "We worked day and night the first year that we were here. I raised a good garden, beans, turnips, peas and sweet potatoes. I canned my vegetables in tin cans which I lined with paper and sealed with sealing wax."[14] Georgia Hancock, her parents,

[10] Interviews of Mrs. W. P. Hickman, 92:459; B. F. Pyne, 93:521–524, IPH; Berthrong, *Cheyenne and Arapaho Ordeal*, 191–192; interview of Annie I. Timmons, 112:246–247, IPH.

[11] Interview of H. W. Slatten, 101:470, IPH.

[12] Interviews of Anna L. Green, 84:369; James Allen Stubbs, 87:441–443, IPH.

[13] Interviews of Anna L. Green, 84:365; Mrs. U. T. Shanley, 101:215, IPH.

[14] Interview of Annie I. Timmons, 112:246, IPH.

Figure 28. At the beginning of the twentieth century, a group of Roger Mills County children attended this frame and stone school. *Oklahoma Historical Society*

and sisters had been on their homestead near Arapaho in Custer County for two years when her father died. "It made it awfully hard on Mother with all of us children," Georgia remembered. "But Mother and I kept on hauling water to sell and took in washings. I went to the field and plowed. We managed to get by and Mother proved up on the claim. . . ."[15]

Medical emergencies were yet another challenge to homesteader families, in part because of the scarcity of doctors in western Oklahoma. Malnutrition and settler living conditions in crowded tents and dugouts probably contributed to illnesses. Bachelor Robert E. Gillian learned immediately that fleas—and to a lesser extent tarantulas, centipedes, and rattlesnakes—besieged dugout dwellers. "I thought I had everything fixed up nicely," he said of his new home near present Elk City, "when I found out that the fleas were so thick I couldn't stay in my bed. I then went out and cut some poles and took some wire and swung the poles to the top of the dugout and fixed my bed up on them out of the reach of the fleas."[16]

According to F. D. Sutton, homesteaders had only been in the vicinity of Old Doxey for three weeks when children in two families

[15] Interview of Georgia Hancock, 92:173, IPH.

[16] Interview of Robert E. Gillian, 80:135, IPH.

58

Figure 29. Homesteaders believed in education. By 1893 Little Robe School, a half dugout, served Dewey County students. *Oklahoma Historical Society.*

sickened with diphtheria. Both children had died by the time a rider brought the nearest doctor from Mangum, forty miles away. Soon there were six small graves in the new Doxey Cemetery. Robert Gillian also recalled a smallpox epidemic in 1899 in the neighborhood of Crow Post Office in the southeast corner of old Roger Mills County. In an effort to prevent its spread, residents drew a quarantine line. Merchant Bob Keen served his customers by throwing their groceries across the line.[17] With rattlesnakes common in western Oklahoma, settlers learned to be careful. J. C. Gilbreath described snakebite treatment he witnessed: "The doctor cut a gash both ways and filled his mouth full of tobacco and sucked the wound. Then he put soda and turpentine on the wound."[18] Mrs. W. P. Hickman experienced a treatment that combined folk medicine and medical practice when a mad dog bit one of her children soon after they settled near Weatherford. "I didn't know what to do," she remembered, "but my husband went to Elk City and learned that there were two mad stones there, one of which was owned by a widow woman who told us that if the stone stuck to the wound it would cost us $2.50; if not, we were to pay nothing. Doctor Clark came to our home and used it and it stuck forty-eight hours."[19]

Rattlesnakes were only some of the creatures in a land rich in animal life. The buffalo were gone, but there were still abundant

[17] Interviews of F. D. Sutton, 87:491–492; Robert E. Gillian, 80:136, IPH.

[18] Interview of J. C. Gilbreath, 84:165, IPH.

[19] Interview of Mrs. W. P. Hickman, 92:492, IPH.

deer, prairie chickens, rabbits, and turkeys. They helped feed hungry families, as did the fish in the waterways. Fishing also offered recreation. Anna L. Green retained good memories of going with friends from their homesteads near Old Doxey to the Washita River to fish. They would camp for a day or two and cook the fish they caught on the bank. Cheyennes and Arapahos enjoyed eating the land turtles that were abundant in western Oklahoma, but homesteaders never seemed to adopt them as a food source.[20]

However, settlers did gather, preserve, and use the same wild fruits Anglo-American explorers had praised in the 1820s and 1830s—wild grapes and plums.[21] According to Anna L. Green, they were the only fruit settlers had. Anna said,

> We didn't have any jars and no money to buy them so I would put the plums on the stove and cook them, then run them through a colander. Then I would put them in tin pans and set them on the chicken house in the sun to dry. When one side would get dry I would take a knife and turn the plums over. When they got dry they were just like rubber. We would sack them up and when we wanted fruit we would put some of this on the stove in some water and it wouldn't be long until they would be dissolved. Then I would put in some sugar and soon there would be some real nice plum butter.[22]

Often, however, homesteaders had little to eat except bread and water gravy. Thinking of life on her Dewey County claim in 1892, Mrs. U. T. Shanley recalled, "Many a time we sat down to eat corn bread and drink some water or maybe we would have some wild plum juice. The other neighbors had no more than we so we did not feel badly about it."[23]

What they had, they were willing to share. Julie Ann Morgan, thinking about how scarce money and work were in Roger Mills County in 1899, believed her family would not have made it "if it had not been for a good old pioneer neighbor giving us something to eat until we could get something raised."[24]

Anna L. Green recalled how neighbors came from miles around in the summer of 1900 when a visiting preacher from Weatherford held a revival on their claim.

> I fed many a person when I didn't know where our next meal was coming from. I would set my dough in the morning and go to preaching. When I came in to cook dinner I would make the dough out into loaves and put it in pans and we would eat dinner and by that time it had risen enough to put in the oven. I would fill the stove full of cow chips, then we would go to a baptizing, for there surely were lots of people baptized, and when we came home in the evening our bread would be done and we would make coffee and water gravy and eat supper.[25]

[20] Interview of Anna L. Green, 84:367, IPH.

[21] Interview of Julie Ann Morgan, 81:106, IPH.

[22] Interview of Anna L. Green, 84:368–369, IPH.

[23] Interview of Mrs. U. T. Shanley, 101:208, IPH.

[24] Interview of Julie Ann Morgan, 81:105, IPH.

[25] Interview of Anna L. Green, 84:367, IPH.

Figure 30. Many homesteaders in western Oklahoma raised cotton on their Washita River Valley lands.
Oklahoma Historical Society

When they had time and energy, settlers made their own entertainment. Mrs. U. T. Shanley looked back on the summer of 1892, the first they spent in Dewey County, when the neighbors decided to go to a dance at Cantonment.

> The men hitched a team of oxen to a wagon and drove as far as we could. There were no roads and we got into a sandy and rocky place where we could not go any farther. There were about seven grown ones in the party and two children. We found some big flat rocks and the oxen were unhitched and turned out to graze. Then as one of the men had a French harp and could play real well, we danced on the red rock floor by the light of the moon. We sure had a good time. I remember that I had on some of those moccasins made from overall legs and wore them out that night dancing on the rocks. We did not get back home until daylight. But we had a lot of fun.[26]

Similarly, Anna Green recalled her family's first Christmas at Old Doxey. Anna and her sister-in-law Minnie walked nine miles across empty prairie to the nearest store to buy presents for their husbands, who were away from home, and three children. But the tiny store had nothing suitable, so they bought a cigar for each husband and stick candy for the children. On the nine-mile walk back, Minnie suffered from blistered heels, so they were very late getting home. Anna said,

[26] Interview of Mrs. U. T. Shanley, 101: 214, IPH.

Figure 31. Five generations of Collier Tracy's family have farmed their homestead in the Washita River Valley. *Oklahoma Historical Society*

The next day Minnie and I went down into a canyon and cut a hackberry tree and dragged it in and dug a hole down in the dirt floor and put it up. This hackberry tree had the berries on it, so we popped corn and strung it over the tree, put the cigars and candy and the children's old toys on the tree, for there were no new ones. We wrapped the tree with a sheet and had it all ready when the men got home. One of them acted as Santa Claus and gave out the gifts. This was our first Christmas in the Territory and was the happiest Christmas of my life.[27]

The homesteaders who stuck it out showed remarkable fortitude in the face of poor shelter, scanty food, little money, and the sheer hard labor of pioneering. Looking back through the haze of memory in the late 1930s, four or five decades later, Cheyenne and Arapaho Reservation homesteaders were proud that they had endured the hard times with optimism that they would succeed in building new lives and homes in a sometimes unwelcoming land. H. W. Slatten, who had come to Washita County from Georgia with a wife, five children, and empty pockets, proudly said, "I now own six hundred and ten acres of land and the way I got it, I dug it out of the ground. I owe no man a penny though I am all 'stove' up from hard work and being out in all kinds of weather. . . ." Slatten pondered, "I don't see how we made it through the hard times but God helped us get by. My wife would cry and cry to go back to Georgia, but I would say to her, 'Lizza, hold your horses. We will come out on top.'"[28]

[27] Interview of Anna L. Green, 84:364–365, IPH.

[28] Interview of H. W. Slatten, 101:471–472, IPH.

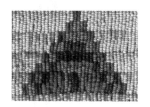

Chapter 6

SHARING THE LAND

The homesteading process in far western Oklahoma continued from the opening in 1892 through about 1912. Drought cycles, lack of good transportation, and conflict over land use between home-steading farmers and cattlemen retarded full settlement of the west-ern half of the former reservation for nearly a decade. Homesteaders generally planned to raise cotton, corn, and wheat on their 160–acre claims, but cattlemen were convinced that western Oklahoma's arid grasslands were only fit for grazing livestock. Cattlemen used warn-ings, intimidation, and sometimes violence to press their point. The passage of herd laws about 1900 ended open-range grazing and pro-tected the crops of farmers from hungry cattle. Passage of the Free Homes Bill in 1900 lifted another burden by ending payments for homesteads.[1]

When it came to building homes, schools, and churches—all high priorities with the homesteaders—they were on their own. But the Oklahoma territorial legislature had already divided the former reservation into counties. Among them were Day and Roger Mills counties. Day County, with its seat at Ioland and later Grand, disap-peared at statehood in 1907, its lands incorporated into Roger Mills and Ellis counties. Numerous towns and communities, usually mar-ket centers for farmers and ranchers, were founded throughout the former reservation. These included Durham, Crawford, Cuthbert, Downey, Roll, Rome, Progress, Shirley, Grow, Angora, Brantley, and Texmo in the north. In the Washita River Valley were Ham-burg, Redmoon, Cheyenne, Strong City, Herring, and Hammon. To the south were Rankin, Harrington, Dempsey, Carpenter, Sweet-water, and Berlin. Most of these towns dwindled away unless nour-ished by the slowly expanding rail system.

Cheyenne, the town nearest Washita Battlefield National His-toric Site, lacked railroad connections but survived as the Roger Mills County seat and a market center for ranchers and farmers in the upper Washita River Valley (See Map 6). When the railroad fi-nally came through Roger Mills County in 1910, it passed through Hammon farther down the Washita River Valley. Cheyenne's citi-zens then raised the money to build their own short line by 1914.

[1] Warde, *Draft Report, Phase IV*, 53–56.

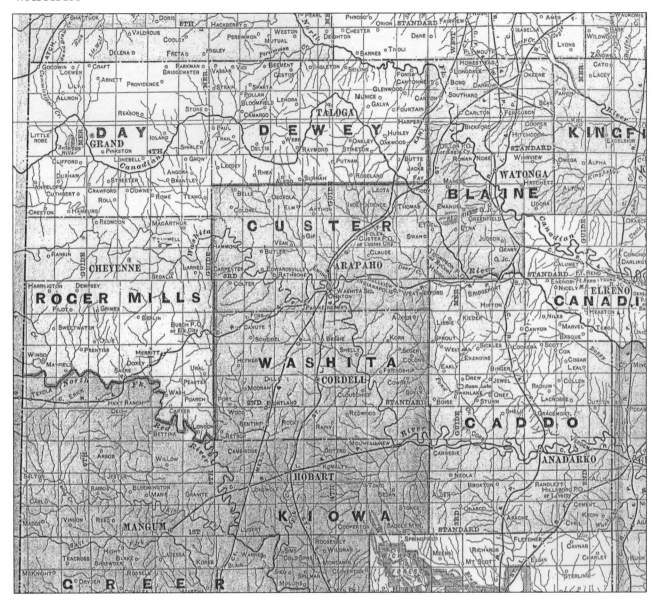

Map 6. A portion of a 1906 map shows the counties designated by the Oklahoma territorial legislature before the land run into the Cheyenne and Arapaho Reservation in 1892. Included are Day County (1892–1907) and a number of small towns and communities established in the first decade after the opening.[2]

[2] *Standard Atlas of Woods County, Oklahoma* (Chicago: George A. Ogle and Company, 1906), Oklahoma Historical Society, Oklahoma City, Oklahoma.

[3] Warde, *Draft Report, Phase IV*, 32–33.

Similarly, Reydon appeared and Rankin disappeared with railroad construction in 1928.[3]

Some experimentation was necessary to discover which crops would flourish in the upper Washita River Valley. Corn, kaffir corn, broomcorn, sorghum, cotton, and wheat were the primary crops for many farmers, but almost all kept livestock as well—horses for transportation and to power farm machinery, along with cows for food and milk. Many farmers made land payments by selling eggs, cream,

Figure 32. Cheyenne, Oklahoma Territory, in 1899. *Oklahoma Historical Society*

and turkeys. The German-Russian farmers who settled primarily in Blaine and Washita counties raised the winter wheat familiar to them from their days in Russia, but other farmers in the Washita River Valley grew cotton as their cash crop. All were at the mercy of fluctuating crop prices and the unpredictable weather.[4]

By the 1930s the character of the area around Washita Battlefield National Historic Site was firmly established. It was rural and agricultural, but the people of Roger Mills County demonstrated two somewhat surprising characteristics: a high degree of appreciation for culture and an inclination toward radicalism in politics. In 1914 Roger Mills County elected Socialists to its entire county governing board and as county judge, assessor, treasurer, and weigher. With Dewey, Beckham, Kiowa, and Major counties, Roger Mills County also elected a Socialist state legislator. This may not have been surprising considering the Socialist platform of the day and the agricultural economy of the county. Also, given that the county population was almost entirely white, Protestant, native born, and at least partially of Southern origin, it was perhaps not unexpected that the Ku Klux Klan was active there from 1922 to 1927. Interest in literature and the arts went beyond the usual pioneer social gatherings. The Savage family of Hammon and Cheyenne were all musicians as well as writers for the local newspapers. Mignon Laird from Cheyenne gained a national reputation as an entertainer in the pre–World War II era. Della Cann Young, who lived west of Cheyenne in the Washita River Valley, was named Oklahoma's fourth poet laureate. And Augusta Metcalfe, widely known for her ability as a fiddler, was a talented painter of western scenes, whose work gained a national audience through *Life Magazine*.[5]

Cheyennes and Arapahos found themselves a very small, often impoverished, and barely tolerated minority in their former reservation. While most settlers were from neighboring Kansas, Texas, and

[4] Ibid., 58–60.

[5] Von Russell Creel, "Socialists in the House: The Oklahoma Experience, Part 1, *The Chronicles of Oklahoma* 70 (Summer 1992):144–183; Klina E. Casady, *Once Every Five Years: A History of Cheyenne, Oklahoma, 1892–1972* (Oklahoma City: Metro Press, 1974), 61; interview of Olena Belle Savage Crane, by Mary Jane Warde, Cheyenne, Oklahoma, February 19,2002 , in Warde, *Draft Report, Phase IV*; interview of Lorena Males, February 20, 2002, ibid.; Melvin Harrell, "'My Life in the Indian Territory of Oklahoma': The Story of Augusta Corson Metcalfe," *The Chronicles of Oklahoma* 33 (Spring 1955):59; interview of Howard Metcalfe, by Rodger Harris, Elk City, Oklahoma, April 12, 1992.

Figure 33. Augusta Corson Metcalfe——homesteader, rancher, fiddler, and artist—painted scenes from her experiences in the Washita River Valley. *Oklahoma Historical Society*

Missouri, there was a very small population of African-American settlers along the eastern edge. A somewhat larger population of German immigrants from Russia colonized parts of Blaine and Washita counties.[6]

Members of western Oklahoma tribes interviewed during this project often continued to live within the boundaries of their former reservations through the twentieth century. Common experiences included making the transition from childhood in a traditional extended family to public or boarding schools, some degree of discrimination from Anglo-American neighbors, low income levels, military service, tribal factionalism, and sorrow for loss of traditional ways, particularly the ability to speak one's tribal language.[7]

Substantial Cheyenne communities existed at Canton and Watonga in Blaine County, Clinton in Custer County, and Hammon in Roger Mills County. Interviews revealed that some traditional communal life and ceremonial ways continued throughout the former reservation and into the mid-twentieth century, particularly in the White Shield community (formerly the Red Moon band) near Hammon. Edwin Pewo, born in 1934, recalled that the community lived off the land, picking plums and mulberries, hunting rabbits, quail, and wild turkeys, and fishing in the river for turtles and catfish.[8] He said,

> I was raised along the river, what they call the White Shield camp . . . I think I was fortunate, very fortunate being able to [have] lived along the Washita White Shield camp with all the

[6] Warde, *Draft Report, Phase IV*, 43–47.

[7] Interview of Laird Cometsevah, by Loretta Fowler, Clinton, Oklahoma, March 9, 2001, in Fowler, *Final Report, Phase II*, 93. See also interviews in Fowler, *Final Report, Phase II*, and Warde, *Final Report, Phase I*.

[8] Interview of Edwin Pewo, by Loretta Fowler, Hammon, Oklahoma, April 4, 2001, in Fowler, *Final Report, Phase II*, 144, 148–149, 152.

elders that was there at the time. More or less, it was just like one big happy family. . . . We didn't have no electricity, no running water, no gas. People cooked with cook stoves. During the wintertime we had to chop wood for the heater, big heater stove, the cook stove. They always had holiday committee, which consisted of Christmas. We had a big hall down there. They used to have hand games, they had dances . . . I really did like that. . . . We never had to worry about no bills, pay or bill-paying, or people coming at you. . . . Sometimes I think about and reminisce about that, but I miss it.[9]

Moses Starr, another White Shield camp resident, also remembered a good life along the Washita River:

I spent so much time along there that I knew every tree, I knew where all the berries were, the plum bushes and where it was good fishing. I used to be able to go fishing because at that time it was really nice. . . . There was perch and there was catfish, and in the river you had different kinds of fish, you know, like channel cat—they're catfish, and also the flathead; they're all in that catfish [family], with the mud cats that were also catfish. Also we took the time to find out exactly where we could go fishing—and we ate that fish, we didn't throw any of it away. Even the small ones, what they would do, they would boil them. They would…boil them with the head on and everything. After they boiled then it was easy to take them off. But the large ones, you know, you could fillet them and fry them.

. . . We did a lot of hunting . . . we used to go possum hunting. And we'd eat them possum; they taste just like pork. They were good with sweet potatoes.

We had a lotta mulberry trees. . . . We used to sit and eat those huckleberries, little bitty brown. They're small and their seed, the meat part and the skin around them is not very much, but they taste good. . . . Plums were really good when they came, when they got ripe. There were two types. One was the sand plums, these plums that you see alongside the road now.

I think that probably all those plums were really great because you could make jam and jelly, you could also dry them. They would make cakes out of them after they'd dry. They'd even mash the seeds after they got them and they left the seeds in them. During the wintertime when you got ready [you put] flour in there and kinda make a plum gravy out of it. Then there was a pudding, what we say pudding is. . . . Currants were really plentiful, but they also were small. So everybody would go along the creek and they'd just sit there and eat them, you know, and enjoy it. . . .[10]

Another one that I forgot was the grapes. They're not that large, just as big as my thumb, you know. They were real small but

[9] Ibid., 145.

[10] Interview of Moses Starr, by Loretta Fowler, Weatherford, Oklahoma, March 26, 2001, in ibid., 159–161.

they grew in bunches—and you had to beat the birds to them. . . . I used to know, along that river, almost every place where they had these grapevines, wild grapevines. And we'd all go down there to see if they were ripe. Those things were really important to the Indian people; you might say they were nourishing. You'd have wild potatoes and you'd have wild onions. . . .

You have several different kinds of turtles.... Along the Washita . . . they have soft shell turtles and you can always see them. What they do, they clean them after they get them. They're fast, they're quick. After you get them they boiled them and after they're done you can pull them apart and all that meat...you can pull the leg and it's got nothing but meat on it and you eat that. And the shell . . . you can eat that. You put salt on it and you can eat the shell; it's soft. . . . The snapping turtle is good to eat. . . . We used to get a lot of those snapping turtles. Those things have maybe sometimes . . . seventy-five eggs. . . . Everybody is grabbing for those eggs. Yeah those were all good to eat. . . .

They used to go out and hunt for [land] turtles, bring in a bunch of them and they'd also clean them and put them in the oven.[11]

Moses Starr also recalled that the Washita River was a good place to break horses:

We'd take them down the river, and that river...it was wide and it was pretty deep, so we used to break horses in there. We'd take them in there and ride them—they couldn't buck. Maybe they'd try to buck two or three times, that water would keep them from getting tired. We'd continue until they quit, 'til they'd come on shore and they wouldn't be bucking. Maybe it'd take two days, three days to really calm them down.[12]

While Cheyennes used traditional knowledge to make the best of living in the Washita River Valley, their Anglo-American neighbors were still learning how to do it. Part of the problem for farmers and ranchers was the unpredictable climate. A 1963 Soil Conservation Service study of Roger Mills County noted, "Precipitation in the county varies so widely from year to year that it is misleading to state that a certain amount of precipitation is 'normal.'"[13] The county was settled primarily from 1905 to 1909, years during which rainfall was plentiful. But drought struck the county in 1910, 1916, 1917, 1918, 1921, 1925, 1929, 1930, 1933, 1934, 1935, and 1936. Twelve times in thirty years drought was so severe the Oklahoma Conservation Commission estimated that crop yields decreased 50 percent or more.[14]

Manuel Hensley, whose family homesteaded in the Washita River Valley near Strong City in 1898, remembered the 1920s when

11 Ibid., March 28, 2001, in ibid., 168–172.

12 Ibid., March 26, 2001, in ibid., 161.

13 Dent L. Burgess, Joe D. Nichols, and Odos G. Henson, *Roger Mills County, Oklahoma*, United States Department of Agriculture, Soil Conservation Service, Survey Bulletin 59, August 1963, 1.

14 Ibid, 3; Oklahoma Conservation Commission, *Biennial Report*, vol. 1, January 15, 1937, 7, 10.

Figure 34. Cotton helped Elk City prosper in 1905, but drought in the 1930s caused many cotton farmers to lose their land. *Oklahoma Historical Society*

the surrounding countryside was checker-boarded with 40–, 80–, and 160–acre farms. With a couple of cows, some chickens, and a kitchen garden, a family could raise enough cotton to get by even on a 40–acre farm. Strong City was a bustling town one mile square with three churches and a three-block-long business district. Long lines of wagons waited for service at three gins. But farm prices began to decline at the end of World War I, and by the 1930s the price of cotton dropped from twenty cents to seven cents per pound in the bale. Then the extended drought of the 1930s set off the Dust Bowl on the high plains of western Oklahoma and surrounding states. Hensley remembered cultivating his father's cotton and finding dry soil five to six inches deep. Asked why they were cultivating with the dirt that dry, his father could only answer that stirring the soil around the plants might help them survive. With no rain, the little sand hills along the valley eroded easily in the dry wind. Hensley summed up what happened to many of his neighbors and their farms: "When the drought came, they had to give it up. They couldn't live off it."[15]

For cattlemen, the 1930s were equally difficult. Billy Chalfant, a rancher on land adjacent to Washita Battlefield National Historic

[15] Interview of Manuel Hensley, by Mary Jane Warde, Strong City, Oklahoma, October 16, 2002, in Warde, *Draft Report, Phase IV*, 62–63.

Figure 35. An upstream dam program helped control erosion in the Washita River Valley. *Oklahoma Historical Society*

Site, remembered, "It was terrible. That's all you can say for it, it was terrible. Drought, you know, and no rain, no nothing. It wasn't anything like it is now. . . . You see grass everywhere and you see water everywhere and you see good fences, good improvements." But then, there were "Little old sorry fences and maybe a little old pond—and they was dry half the time. 'Cause creeks and rivers, they'd go dry and we'd scrape water." Using a slip, or fresno, ranchers scraped out a hole which was filled with water that soon evaporated. Chalfant commented, "Got to be awful nasty water for cattle to drink, but that's all they had."[16]

Ranchers were forced to sell or destroy cattle they could not water or feed. Collier Tracy, who ranched in the Washita River Valley west of Cheyenne, remembered the pain of selling his cattle for two or three dollars a head.[17] Clara King Davis remembered, "The grass in the pasture crunched under our feet, and it hadn't rained for over a year." She helped her father and brother drive thirty cows to a canyon to be shot. The government paid her father four dollars a head for the cattle, but Clara "saw tears trickling down her father's face as the cows were shot."[18]

Those who could no longer live on the land moved away. The population of Roger Mills County, which had fluctuated in the past, peaked in 1930 at 14,164 and then began a steady decline. Strong City, according to Manuel Hensley, saw many leave. The town, which had a population of 353 in 1930 dwindled to 245 in 1940.[19] But others stayed and found a way to keep going. Hensley summed it

[16] Interview of Billy Chalfant, by Mary Jane Warde, Cheyenne, Oklahoma, July 9, 2002, in ibid., 63.

[17] Interview of Dale Tracy, Collier Tracy, and Judy Tracy, by the Mary Jane Warde, Cheyenne, Oklahoma, vicinity, July 9, 2002, in ibid.

[18] Clara King Davis, *The Winds of Change on Croton Creek* (Stillwater, Okla.: New Forums Press, 1997), 94.

[19] U. S. Bureau of the Census, Population of Counties by Decennial Census, 1900–1990, Oklahoma, retrieved February 21, 2003, from http://www.census.gov/population/cencounts/ok199090.txt; INTERNET.

Figure 36. Dale Tracy stands next to a buffalo wallow marked by vegetation. Eroded lands north of the Washita Battlefield are visible in the background. *Oklahoma Historical Society*

up, "Them old farmers were tough, you know. Them old ranchers, they could stand it and they survived."[20]

Survival took various forms. Lester Davis, from a family of cotton farmers, left school for a year to join the Civilian Conservation Corps. He worked on soil conservation projects, primarily building spillways for newly terraced hillsides. Asked how people got along with so little income, he stated succinctly, "They didn't spend much money." The family of his future wife, Clara King, held on to Bar Z Ranch on Croton Creek west of Cheyenne by breaking horses for five or ten dollars a head. The Kings also milked twenty-five Herefords, range cattle rather than dairy cows, but "You used what you had."[21] Their garden produced tomatoes, green beans, and two wagon loads of cabbages that sold well in the new town of Reydon. The money went to pay interest on their land mortgages.[22]

L. L. "Red" Males, a bank loan officer in Cheyenne, was especially concerned about the situation in the Washita River Valley. He knew farmers and ranchers were having difficulty repaying loans, but he was also disturbed by the damage the drought was doing to the land. His wife Lorena remembered, "He'd look out the window, the big glass window, and see the Dust Bowl, the dirt blowing. Sometimes he'd come home and couldn't eat his lunch, he'd be so worried about what that dust was doing. He said, 'If we lose our soil, we're

[20] Interview of Manuel Hensley, in Warde, *Draft Report, Phase IV*, 63.

[21] Interview of Clara King Davis and R. Davis, by Mary Jane Warde, Cheyenne, Oklahoma vicinity, October 16, 2002, in ibid., 64.

[22] Davis, *Winds of Change*, 94.

Figure 37. Flood control benefitted farmers in the Washita River Valley. *Oklahoma Historical Society*

lost; there's nothing for any of us.'"[23] Ironically, in the midst of the Dust Bowl, the Washita River Valley suffered a devastating flood.

Spring floods on the Washita were fairly common, but no one had seen anything like this. On April 13, 1934, after two wet days, the clouds piled up and heavy rains moved in from the north. In five hours 13.79 inches fell, and the deluge washed away soil left thinly covered and vulnerable by the drought. By the time the flood reached Hammon, it was a wall of water some eighteen feet high sweeping everything out of its way. The "Hammon flood," as it was known locally, drowned nineteen people, including one whole family, and washed out wide sections of the railroad bed. Eventually the flood, scouring out the riverbed and moving the earth elsewhere, made its way downstream through Butler and Clinton. Manuel Hensley had disposed of his old car by pushing it into the riverbed. When the water went down, its three-foot high tires were buried in silt.[24]

L. L. Males and other activists began a lobbying effort to inform state and federal legislators about the extent of wind and water erosion in western Oklahoma, particularly Roger Mills County. Through New Deal legislation from 1933 to 1937, the federal government purchased tax-delinquent, abandoned lands near the Oklahoma-Texas Panhandle border, now incorporated into Black Kettle National Grassland. The Soil Conservation Service began rehabilitation of these lands in 1939 by controlling grazing and replanting grass. The late 1940s saw the creation of the nation's first upstream flood control project in the Sandstone Creek watershed in southeastern Roger Mills County. Farmers and ranchers in the Washita River Valley could now confidently use lands once subject to frequent flooding. Residents today still regard the combination of erosion and

[23] Interview of Lorena Males, February 20, 2002, in Warde, *Draft Report, Phase IV*, 64.

[24] Casady, *Once Every Five Years*, 70–77; interview of Manuel Hensley, October 16, 2002, in Warde, *Draft Report, Phase IV*, 65; Marjorie Savage Heeney, "Cheyenne Memories," *Cheyenne* (Oklahoma) *Star*, April 19, 1990.

Figure 38. Today, crops grow where Indian camped. *Oklahoma Historical Society*

flood control in the "little dams" project one of the greatest federal benefits to the county. Black Kettle National Grassland, which surrounds Washita Battlefield National Historic Site, brought additional benefits by restoring the wildlife population and creating recreational opportunities on new lakes.[25]

Rainfall and prosperity returned in the 1940s and 1950s, but life in the vicinity of Washita Battlefield National Historic Site changed very little. The area remained primarily rural and agricultural, with farmers and ranchers producing cattle, wheat, and other small grains. With improved transportation, there was less need for market centers. Consequently, the number of towns dwindled, leaving Cheyenne and Hammon the primary towns in Roger Mills County. More and more young people left to make their lives elsewhere. There was a brief oil boom in the 1980s, but it passed quickly, and the pace of life slowed again as oil field workers moved on.[26]

Life also changed for the Cheyennes. Earlier in the twentieth century Cheyenne children attended public and boarding schools such as Concho, Canton, Seger, and Red Moon, before going on to Chilocco Indian School or to Haskell Institute in Lawrence, Kansas. Although the experience could be harsh, some credited skills learned at the last two as having prepared them to earn a livelihood in a world dominated by Anglo-Americans. Many of the men and some women served in the armed forces during World War II, the Korean Conflict, and the Vietnam War. They and their communities still take pride in their military service, demonstrated in the revived warrior societies and veterans' organizations. Some made careers in the armed forces and the Indian Service. After decades of attempting to extinguish tribalism, the federal government reversed its policies

[25] Ibid., 66, 68; "Black Kettle and McClellan Creek," retrieved June 4, 2003, from http://www.fs.fed.us/r2/nebraska/gpng/blmc.html; INTERNET.

[26] Warde, *Draft Report, Phase IV,* 68–72.

during the administration of New Deal Commissioner of Indian Affairs John Collier. The Cheyenne and Arapaho Tribes emerged as one of many Indian governments as Indian sovereignty regained federal recognition. However, the traditional Council of Forty-four chiefs also functioned on an unofficial but important level. The revival of the Sun Dance, renewal of the Medicine Arrows, and adoption of the Native American Church along with Indian Christianity provided an anchor and an Indian way of coping with the difficulties of life in the twentieth century. The powwow, an intertribal movement that emerged in the 1930s and 1940s, also reinforced Indian identity. As Laird Cometsevah said, "This Arrow Tepee . . . it always draws the Cheyennes back together, their what you would say unity—it keeps them together, our Indian ways, our Arrow Tepee, our ceremonies, our what they call powwows nowadays, our source of entertainment on the Indian way. This keeps our people united, holding on to our Indian ways."[27]

The White Shield camp near Hammon disappeared in the 1950s. Edwin Pewo remembered that while he served in Korea and the peacetime military, "these people [in the White Shield camp], each one, they gradually sold their land, come to town, bought a home. Every one of them that happened, all of them they all left that place down there. . . . So everybody just left, tore all the old houses down, burned them down. Now nobody lives out there anymore."[28]

Life has not been easy for the Cheyennes and Arapahos. Joe Osage, a Cheyenne minister interviewed in 1999 about life among Hammon Cheyennes, noted that few Cheyenne students stayed in high school long enough to graduate and many left the community to find work elsewhere. On the other hand, some interviewees spoke proudly of children and grandchildren who had earned university degrees and now had promising careers.[29] Rollin Haag summarized, "We are all aware of the history of our ancestors, and for the most part, while we have lived fairly successful and decent lives, under the guidance of our spirituality of our ancestors by the advice we should accept life on life's terms for the sake of those that are coming in the future, and because they deserve a chance at this life."[30]

[27] See interviews in Fowler, *Draft Report, Phase III*, and Warde, *Final Report, Phase I.*

[28] Interview of Edwin Pewo, April 4, 2001, in Fowler, *Draft Report, Phase III*, 152.

[29] Interview of Lorena Savage Males, February 20, 2002, in Warde, *Draft Report, Phase IV*; Glen Crane, "Indians," *Cheyenne* (Oklahoma) *Star*, April 19, 1990; interview of Joe Osage, by Mary Jane Warde and Jim Anquoe, Hammon, Oklahoma, September 1, 1999 in Warde, *Final Report, Phase I.*

[30] Interview of Rollin Haag, by Loretta Fowler, Calumet, Oklahoma, December 18, 2002, in Fowler, *Final Report, Phase II*, 130.

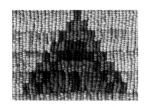

Chapter 7

REMEMBERING WASHITA

The Washita Massacre, or Battle of the Washita, offered a point of contact between Cheyennes and their Anglo-American neighbors. But the question was, how should it be remembered? Attempts began as early as 1910 among the residents of Cheyenne, Oklahoma, to mark the site. Interest was somewhat cyclical as local leadership and interest fluctuated. The erection of a marker, reenactments, the establishment of Black Kettle Museum, and the movement for designation of the battlefield as a National Historic Site marked periodic high points of interest among the residents of Roger Mills County.[1]

However, the meanings and intentions of commemorating the event and site often varied widely between Cheyennes and Anglo-Americans. From the first efforts of Cheyenne, Oklahoma's Anglo-American citizens in 1910, commemoration of the Seventh Cavalry attack on Chief Black Kettle's camp was incorporated into celebrations of Anglo-American pioneer heritage in western Oklahoma. Invitations to the Cheyenne community at Hammon to participate were not always successful. Cheyennes who survived the attack were still living in the 1920s and 1930s. They recalled the trauma of an event they viewed as a massacre, which did not quite fit the heroic pioneer heritage concept. The centennial reenactment in 1968 was particularly disturbing for some Cheyennes who understood their history and recalled it with bitterness.[2]

At the same time, Cheyennes and Anglo-Americans sometimes differed on the practical outcome of commemoration. Given the chronic decline in population in Roger Mills County and few economic opportunities available in the somewhat isolated rural setting, Anglo-Americans saw reenactments, establishment of Black Kettle Museum, and creation of Washita Battlefield National Historic Site as spurs toward potential economic growth and development. Even though there was a strong degree of local non-Indian skepticism about development, some saw tourism as a highly favorable thing for the future of Roger Mills County.[3]

While Washita Battlefield supporters related it to enhanced tourism, Cheyennes interviewed during this project saw the location as sacred ground hallowed by their ancestors' deaths. Contemporary

[1] Warde, *Draft Report, Phase IV*, 72–75.

[2] Interviews of Lawrence Hart, by Mary Jane Warde and Rodger Harris, Oklahoma City, Oklahoma, January 14, 1999; Lucille Youngbull, by Mary Jane Warde, Clinton, Oklahoma, July 29, 1999; Larry Roman Nose, by Mary Jane Warde, El Reno, Oklahoma, May 12, 1999, in Warde, *Final Report, Phase I*.

[3] Interview of Judy Tracy, by Mary Jane Warde, Cheyenne, Oklahoma vicinity, July 9, 2002, in Warde, *Draft Report, Phase IV*.

75

Figure 39. Eagle Nest, aged ninety-four when this portrait was made in 1948, was believed to be the last survivor of the Washita Massacre. *Oklahoma Historical Society*

Cheyennes were unified in the view that the event was a massacre, not a battle, and the name of Washita Battlefield National Historic Site should be changed to reflect that. Eugene Blackbear, Sr., whose ancestors also escaped the Sand Creek Massacre, said,

> When you talk about Battle of Washita, they call it "battle" but it was not a battle. You read the books, you read all these how the Cheyenne told them how they were treated, they were sneaked up on, coming in there at daybreak. Everybody was sleeping, they were surprise attacked, just like Pearl Harbor, Japanese did the Americans. Same tactics was used on our Cheyenne people. So it's difficult today. They're trying to make a big historical landmark. The feelings of some of us, it's good in one way and on the other hand it's sad where so many people were slaughtered. So many children, man, woman, kids, were killed to make a showplace of it.[4]

What happened at Washita Battlefield, according to the interviews collected from Cheyennes during this project, was a link in a chain of events that account in part for their attitudes toward Anglo-Americans. From their perspective, the 1864 Sand Creek Massacre, the Washita Massacre, and the attack on Cheyennes at Palo Duro Canyon were related in that they demonstrated white treach-

[4] Interview of Eugene Blackbear, Sr., by Loretta Fowler, Norman, Oklahoma, September 20, 2000, in Fowler, *Final Report, Phase II*, 84.

Figure 40. A monument marks the site of the Washita Massacre, now Washita Battlefield National Historic Site. *Oklahoma Historical Society*

ery. When Custer ignored the symbolism of the ashes poured on his boots, it assured eventual justice, which came to him in the 1876 Battle of the Little Bighorn. Moreover, in the late twentieth century the chain of treachery extended to include the failure of the federal government to return Fort Reno to the Cheyenne and Arapaho Tribes.[5]

Perhaps Rollin Haag best summed up two divergent views Cheyennes may take toward what happened at the Washita Massacre, its continuing impact on Cheyennes, and what should be interpreted. Remembering the teachings and prophecies of Sweet Medicine, Haag said,

> That's why myself and my relatives, we're still here under that influence and we try to cope, even though we were told about the story of the massacres and we grew up with a lot of anger, my brothers and myself. Some of my brothers could not accept this society and the ways of these European systems that were imposed on us. So some of my brothers chose not to stay here through their own abuse of themselves: alcohol, alcoholism, anger, frustration.

But Haag found comfort and hope in

[5] Interview of Joe Big Medicine, by Loretta Fowler, Watonga, Oklahoma, August 19, 2000, in ibid., 80–81.

The unborn generations, our grandchildren, great-grandchildren. Those were the words of Chief Black Kettle: to pray for our enemies and to forgive them for harming our people, and to pray for them to distribute the truth of love and compassion among our tribal members and to stand side by side behind the principles of truth, and the precious life that we acknowledge from our Creator *Maheo*, the Great Spirit and Supreme Being, the spirit of love and truth.[6]

Looking at this project to collect information about what happened at Washita Battlefield National Historic Site and about the people who have occupied and passed through the site over the centuries, Joe Big Medicine said, "I feel that doing this interview…is very important to our future generation, to the public, on describing events and describing how people feel today, what should happen to the Washita in remembrance of our people, of the Black Kettle village. It shouldn't be erased, it should be recorded, it should be kept, protected and brought out to the public."[7]

Archie Hoffman said, "If you're going to build a national park you need to tell the truth about what happened. The truth has been changed around to make it look like our Indian people were the bad people, like we were the ones killing the white people, when all along the white people were trying to exterminate our Indian people."[8]

Finally, Clara King Davis, a descendant of the Cherokee Ballard family whose ancestors homesteaded west of Washita Battlefield National Historic Site, agreed that the truth must be told. She hoped, "that they will present it in a historical fashion, as part of our history, and surely we have to live with whatever we did in our history." She continued, "For us to know how to go on in our future, I think we have to know where we come from. . . . I hope that in all their discussions they will not try to pit the Indians against the whites, just tell it like it was—we certainly don't need any more prejudice."[9]

[6] Interview of Rollin Haag, by Loretta Fowler, Calumet, Oklahoma, December 18, 2002, in ibid., 129–130.

[7] Interview of Joe Big Medicine, by Loretta Fowler, Watonga, Oklahoma, August 19, 2000, in ibid., 78.

[8] Interview of Archie Hoffman, by Loretta Fowler, September 15, 2002, in ibid., 140.

[9] Interview of Clara King Davis and Lester B. Davis, October 16, 2002, quoted in Warde, *Draft Report, Phase IV*, 75.

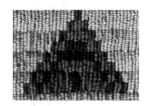

ABOUT THIS PROJECT

As you visit Washita Battlefield National Historic Site (WBNHS), please keep in mind that many peoples have used and occupied this land over the centuries. The objectives of this phase of the Washita Project were to complete comprehensive reports on human association with the land that will be useful to National Park Service staff and to the general public. The reports include:

1. reviews of anthropological and historical literature about the historical and contemporary relationships between the traditional associations of Indian and local non-Indian communities and landowners within the WBNHS area;

2. identification of contemporary people and communities who may retain interest in and traditional associations with lands and resources now encompassed by WBNHS, based on preliminary research.

These reports are intended to supply data for park managers on which to base decisions about resource management, planning, and interpretation. At the same time, it is hoped that the reports will be useful to the general public, adding to their appreciation of the site, and to researchers studying the relationship of peoples to the land over time.

If you are interested in learning more about the site and its history, you will find helpful resources at the Oklahoma Historical Society, the Western History Collections at the University of Oklahoma, Oklahoma State University, the Black Kettle Museum in Cheyenne, Oklahoma, and the Elk City Carnegie Library at Elk City, Oklahoma. Types of resources available in these archives, libraries, and museums include books, journal articles, federal Indian agency records, other federal records and reports, state agency reports, state commission reports, county records, manuscript collections, missionary records, theses, dissertations, newsletters, newspaper articles, vertical files, maps, historic photographs, abstracts, computer databases, Internet sites, and oral histories. Copies of all the Washita Project reports, as well as related National Park Service reports prepared by staff members Jill Cowley and Jerry Greene, are also available to the general public at the Oklahoma Historical Society.[1]

The findings of this study suggest several important points to consider about Washita Battlefield National Historic Site:

1. The location of WBNHS has held significance for several peoples and different cultures over the centuries.
2. Remembering tribal and European names for landscape features aids understanding of the knowledge, use, and importance of the location of WBNHS by a succession of peoples.
3. The location of WBNHS can best be understood in a regional context.
4. Linking it to state and federal historic sites in Texas, Kansas, New Mexico, Arkansas, Colorado, and Oklahoma provides a better historical, geographical, and cultural context.
5. WBNHS has been situated on successive frontiers in the history of the Southern Plains.
6. Although the location seems isolated today, or "off the beaten track" of Interstate 40 and Route 66, it lies very near one of the most-used east-west routes across the Southern Plains before the twentieth century.
7. The Washita Massacre most deeply affected the Cheyennes, but it also had an impact on other tribes located in Oklahoma today.
8. Several tribes believe that they have old claims on the site and a stake in the interpretation of WBNHS.
9. While non-Indian residents of Roger Mills County see WBNHS in terms of economic development, Cheyennes see the site as sacred.
10. For other tribes, the Washita Massacre commemorated at WBNHS symbolizes what they view as the sometimes hostile and unjust relationship of Anglo-Americans and the federal government to Indians.

This project created a unique opportunity to gather in-depth information about a place and an event. The researchers discovered that no comprehensive regional historical study of western Oklahoma existed. In fact, scholarly works on western Oklahoma were usually limited to journal articles or individual tribal histories. Works on the twentieth century were even more rare. While local and county histories represented a vast amount of work and dedication, they were often not documented and therefore of limited usefulness. Although at least three series of interviews of Indian and

[1] Jill Cowley, *Cultural Landscape Inventory, Level Two, Washita Battlefield National Historic Site* (Santa Fe: National Park Service, Intermountain Region, Santa Fe Support Office, 1999); Jerome A. Greene, *Historic Resource Study. Washita Battlefield National Historic Site, Oklahoma* (Denver: [National Park Service], 2001). The latter report is the basis of a book, Jerome A. Greene, *Washita: The U.S. Army and the Southern Cheyennes, 1867–1869* (Norman: University of Oklahoma Press, 2004).

non-Indian residents had been collected in the twentieth century, some had not been transcribed, synthesized, or indexed. The study findings, then, provide an overview of western Oklahoma history that will be helpful to scholars and general readers as well as for interpretation of WBNHS.

While existing physical anthropological and archaeological information may require additional research, ethnographic and ethnohistorical information from which to determine affiliations with WBNHS is plentiful. During the last five years, while this project was under way, NPS staff members Jill Cowley and Jerry Greene, as well as private contractors, were conducting related research projects. Combining and using the results of all these projects greatly enhances the ability of the planners to develop and interpret WBNHS.

Lastly, it is important that all the communities associated with the site be kept informed about concerns, plans, and progress. Frequent community meetings that allow open discussion and contribution of ideas promote the broad ownership of WBNHS that it deserves. While the developers and planners work to preserve the Indian history and oral tradition associated with the event and the site, they should also remember that these are important intellectual properties that deserve to be treated with respect.

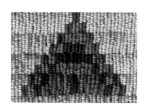

ANNOTATED BIBLIOGRAPHY
Including References Cited

Books, Articles, and Theses

Abel, Annie Heloise. *Tabeau's Narrative of Loisel's Expedition to the Upper Missouri*. Norman: University of Oklahoma Press, 1939.
Tabeau obtained information on the tribes of the Plains while working in the fur trade.

————. "Truteau's Description of the Upper Missouri." *Mississippi Valley Historical Review* 8 (nos. 1–2, 1921):149–179.
Fur trader Truteau traveled up the Missouri River in 1795 obtaining information on Plains tribes.

Anderson, Gary Clayton. *The Indian Southwest, 1580–1830: Ethnogenesis and Reinvention*. Norman: University of Oklahoma Press, 1999.
Based on primary sources, this is a history of social change in the greater Southwest. The book focuses on the ways native societies reorganized over time, developing new social institutions and understandings. The Apache, Caddo, Wichita, and Comanche peoples are discussed.

Baird, W. David. "Cathedrals of the Plains: The Grain Elevators of Western Oklahoma." *The Chronicles of Oklahoma* 70 (Spring, 1992):4–25.
Provides information on wheat production and storage facilities in western Oklahoma.

————. *The Chickasaw People*. Phoenix: Indian Tribal Series, 1974.
Written for a general audience, the book covers the period of European contact up to the present.

Baird, W. David, and Danney Goble. *The Story of Oklahoma*. Norman: University of Oklahoma Press, 1998.
A high school level textbook that incorporates scholarship through the 1990s.

Bass, Althea. *The Arapaho Way: A Memoir of an Indian Boyhood*. New York: C. N. Potter, 1966.
A narrative based on Carl Sweezy's recollections of early reservation days. It focuses on the Arapahos' attempts to accommodate to reservation policy on their own terms.

———. "The Cheyenne Transporter." *The Chronicles of Oklahoma* 46 (Spring, 1968):127–140.
The first newspaper in western Oklahoma was the *Cheyenne Transporter* (1879–1886) of Darlington Agency. It reflected the interests of the Cheyenne Indians as well as cattlemen and the military in the reservation.

Battey, Thomas C. *The Life and Adventures of a Quaker among the Indians.* Williamstown, Mass.: Corner House, 1875, 1972 edition.
Battey was a teacher in the boarding school on the Wichita-Caddo Reservation in 1871.

Baugh, T. G. "Cultural History and Protohistoric Societies in the Southern Plains." In *Current Trends in Southern Plains Archaeology*, ed. T. G. Baugh. *Plains Anthropologist Memoir,* no. 23, 1986.
An interpretation of Southern Plains prehistory most accessible to specialists.

Bell, R. E. "The Plains Villages: The Washita River." In *Prehistory of Oklahoma*, ed. R. E. Bell. Orlando: Academic Press, 1984.
A somewhat dated summary, written for specialists.

———. "Protohistoric Wichita." In *Prehistory of Oklahoma*, ed. R. E. Bell. Orlando: Academic Press, 1984.
A good summary of research on sites that date just prior to the arrival of Europeans.

Bell, Robert E., Edward B. Jelks, and W. W. Newcomb. *Wichita Indian Archaeology and Ethnohistory: A Pilot Study.* In *American Indian Ethnohistory: Plains Indians*, ed. David Agee Horr. New York: Garland Publisher, 1969, 1974 edition.
This description of sites in western Oklahoma and northern Texas is dated and most accessible to specialists.

Bement, Lee, and Kent Buehler. "Bison, Nuts, and the Dempsey Divide." *Oklahoma Archaeological Survey Newsletter* 20 (July 2000):1–3.
This article discusses findings associated with prehistoric bison kill sites on the Dempsey Divide in Beckham County between the North Fork of the Red River and Sandstone Creek.

Beutler, Randy L. "Broncs, Bulls, and Contracts: The Rodeo World of the Beutler Brothers." *The Chronicles of Oklahoma* 63 (Spring, 1985): 48–57.
In 1929 the three Beutler brothers of Custer County entered the rodeo livestock business, playing a major role in the rodeo circuit and western movies. Based on family record and interviews.

Berthrong, Donald J. "Cattlemen on the Cheyenne-Arapaho Reservation, 1883–1885." *Arizona and the West* 3 (Spring, 1971):5–32.
Describes white incursions into the Cheyenne-Arapaho Reservation and conflict that developed between Cheyenne Dog Soldiers, cattlemen, and settlers in neighboring Kansas.

———. *The Cheyenne and Arapaho Ordeal: Reservation and Agency Life in the Indian Territory, 1875–1907*. Norman: University of Oklahoma Press, 1976.

A detailed study based on primary sources of Cheyenne life at the agency from 1875 to 1907. It includes mention of the Red Moon band.

———. "Legacies of the Dawes Act: Bureaucrats and Land Thieves at the Cheyenne-Arapaho Agencies of Oklahoma." *Arizona and the West* 21 (Winter, 1979):335–354.

Describes how legislation from 1902 to 1910 permitting the sale of Indian allotted lands resulted in fraud and dispossession of Cheyennes and Arapahos by white settlers and businessmen.

———. *The Southern Cheyennes*. Norman: University of Oklahoma Press, 1963.

A detailed study based on primary sources of the Cheyennes' early history just prior to their moving onto the Plains to 1875.

———. "White Neighbors Come Among the Southern Cheyenne and Arapaho." *Kansas Quarterly* 3 (no. 4, 1971):105–115.

Discusses the conflicts between the Indians and settlers after the 1892 opening, Indian losses, and the difficulty of Indians obtaining justice.

Bittle, William E. "Manatidie: A Focus for Kiowa Apache Tribal Identity." *Plains Anthropologist* 7 (1962):152–163.

Bittle did the fieldwork for this study in 1959. He argues that the revival of the Blackfeet Society increased social unity and strengthened the sociocultural identity of the Apache.

Bolton, Herbert E., trans. and ed. *Althanase de Mezieres and the Louisiana-Texas Frontier, 1768–1780: Documents Published for the First Time, from the Original Spanish and French Manuscripts*, 2 vols. New York: Cleveland, Ohio: [Arthur H. Clark], 1914.

Mezieres was appointed to administer Louisiana province for the Spanish in 1769. He reports on several councils with Caddos and Wichitas.

———. *The Hasinais: Southern Caddoans as Seen by the Earliest Europeans*. Norman: University of Oklahoma Press, 1987.

Bolton wrote this manuscript based on Spanish and French primary sources. It names and locates the tribes of the Hasinai confederacy and describes aspects of Caddo life between the late seventeenth and late eighteenth centuries: family and kinship, political organization, war, curing, economy, and religion.

Bonnifield, Paul. "Energy Resources on the Southern Great Plains." *The Chronicles of Oklahoma* 59 (Fall, 1981):345–359.

Oil and natural gas exploration and extraction in western Oklahoma and the Texas Panhandle helped maintain prosperity for some communities during the Dust Bowl era of the 1930s.

Botkin, B. A., ed. *Folk-Say: A Regional Miscellany, 1930*. Norman: University of Oklahoma Press, 1930.
This collection of articles includes folkways on a variety of topics and includes an article by Della Cann Young.

Boyd, Maurice. *Kiowa Voices: Ceremonial Dance, Ritual and Song*, vol. 1. Fort Worth: Christian University Press, 1981.
This project involved Kiowa elders and drew on the papers of Susan Peters, who worked on the reservation in the 1930s. There are stories about Kiowa origin tradition and historical events and persons.

———. *Kiowa Voices: Myths, Legends and Folktales*, vol. 2. Fort Worth: Christian University Press, 1983.
See above.

Brant, Charles S. "Kiowa-Apache Culture History: Some Further Observations." *Southwestern Journal of Anthropology* 9 (1953):195–202.
Brant argues for the origin of the Apache in the Southwest and for their affiliation with the Dismal River archaeological tradition.

———. *Jim Whitewolf: The Life of a Kiowa Apache Indian*. New York: Dover, 1969.
A life history recorded in 1948–1949. The book includes a good introduction to the sociocultural organization and history of the Apache.

Brill, Charles J. *Conquest of the Southern Plains: Uncensored Narrative of the Battle of the Washita and Custer's Southern Campaign*. Oklahoma City: Golden Saga Publishers, 1938.
Brill incorporated the recollections of Cheyenne and Arapaho survivors into a historical account of events immediately preceding the massacre and immediately after it. Brill was the first critic of Custer.

———. "The End of the Cheyenne Trail." *The Daily Oklahoman* (Oklahoma City), November 23, 1930.
Memories and comments of Magpie about the Washita Massacre.

Brown, Margaret E. "Homesteading in Roger Mills County: The Wilcox Family." *The Chronicles of Oklahoma* 73 (Summer, 1995):172–190.
Describes the attempt of the Wilcox family—parents and six children—to homestead the "Snakey Bend" of the Canadian River near Grand from 1902 through 1915. The Wilcoxes engaged in threshing and freighting because of the poor farming conditions. Based on oral history and correspondence.

Buntin, Martha L. "History of the Kiowa, Comanche, and Wichita Indian Agency." Master's thesis, University of Oklahoma, 1931.
This is largely a history of the agency and the agents who worked there; the tribes are not distinguished and the documentation is poor.

Carlson, Gustav G., and Volney H. Jones. "Some Uses of Plants by the Comanche Indians." In *Papers of the Michigan Academy of Science, Arts and Letters* 25 (1939):517–542.

This study was based on interviews with Comanches in 1933. The authors identify and discuss the uses of plants for food, medicine, and other purposes.

Carricker, Robert C. *Fort Supply, Indian Territory: Frontier Outpost on the Plains.* Norman: University of Oklahoma Press, 1970.
A study of the military post closest to the Cheyenne and Arapaho Reservation, founded at the time of the Washita Massacre.

Carroll, John M. *General Custer and the Battle of the Washita: The Federal View.* Bryan, Tex.: Guidon Press, 1978.
A collection of military documents concerning events prior to and during the Washita Massacre.

Carter, Cecile Elkins. *Caddo Indians: Where We Come From.* Norman: University of Oklahoma Press, 1995.
Written by a tribal member, this is an account of the Caddos, based on primary sources and interviews that relate the past to the present. It covers early contact to the exodus from Texas.

Carter, Robert Goldthwaite. *On the Border with Mackenzie; or, Winning West Texas from the Comanches.* New York: Antiquarian Press, 1935, 1961 edition.
Carter was an officer under Ranald Mackenzie. His account covers the military campaign against the Comanches, Kiowas, Cheyennes, and Arapahos in the 1870s.

Casady, Klina E. *Once Every Five Years: A History of Cheyenne, Oklahoma, 1892– 1972.* Oklahoma City: Metro Press, 1974.
This book chronicles the events between the pioneer days commemorations, which took place every five years, in Cheyenne, Oklahoma.

———. *A Romance of the Soil: Reclamation of Roger Mills County.* Np., Klina Casady, 1971.
This collection of short articles describes individual contributions to the reclamation of Roger Mills County land following the droughts and floods of the 1930s.

Cash, Joseph H., and Gerald W. Wolff. *The Comanche People.* Phoenix: Indian Tribal Series, 1974.
Written for a general audience, this history covers the period of European contact up to the 1970s.

Catlin, George. *Letters and Notes on the Manners, Customs and Conditions of the North American Indians.* 2 vols. London, 1844.
Catlin traveled through Indian country between 1832 and 1839, writing his observations and painting portraits and scenes of Indian life. He spent time in Comanche camps and visited Kiowas, Wichitas, and Choctaws.

Chalfant, William Y. *Without Quarter: The Wichita Expedition and the Fight on Crooked Creek.* Norman: University of Oklahoma Press, 1991.

A detailed history of military engagements against the Comanches in 1858–1859. Chalfant provides information about individual Comanches and the Wichitas, Caddos, and Delawares who served with the troops.

Chapman, Berlin. "Dissolution of the Wichita Reservation." *The Chronicles of Oklahoma* Part 1, 22 (Summer, 1944):192–207; Part 2 (Fall, 1944):300–314.
Detailed history of the Wichitas' struggle to obtain legal recognition of their land rights in the Washita River Valley. Chapman worked with Wichita tribal members in writing this history.

———. "Establishment of the Wichita Reservation." *The Chronicles of Oklahoma* 11 (Winter, 1933):1044–1053.
Good overview of Wichita efforts to obtain a reservation in their homeland.

Chapman, R. R. "Cheyenne-Arapaho Homestead." *The Chronicles of Oklahoma* 58 (Fall, 1980):343–346.
Reminiscences of a settler couple who homesteaded near Arapaho in Custer County.

Clark, Ben. "Custer's Fight." *Cheyenne* (Oklahoma Territory) *Sunbeam*,. 1899.
Clark was Custer's chief of scouts at the Washita fight and worked at the Cheyenne-Arapaho Agency in subsequent years. He spoke to Cheyenne and Arapaho participants in the fight. He was interviewed by a newspaper reporter some years later.

Cocking, Matthew. "An Adventurer from Hudson Bay: Journal of Matthew Cocking, from York Factory to the Blackfeet Country, 1772–73." In L. Burpee, ed. *Transactions of the Royal Society of Canada.* Third series, vol. 2, 1908:89–121.
Cocking was sent by Hudson's Bay Company to make contact with the nomadic tribes on the upper Saskatchewan and explore trade opportunities.

Collings, Ellsworth. "Roman Nose: Chief of the Southern Cheyenne." *The Chronicles of Oklahoma* 42 (Winter, 1965):429–457.
Henry Roman Nose (1856–1917), who supported peace and education, worked to improve Cheyenne living conditions. He founded the Roman Nose Gypsum Company near Roman Nose State Park in 1906.

Cowley, Jill. *Cultural Landscape Inventory, Level Two, Washita Battlefield National Historic Site.* Santa Fe: National Park Service, Intermountain Region, Santa Fe Support Office, 1999.
A National Park Service study of the use of natural resources in the upper Washita River Valley.

Crane, Glen. "Indians." *The Cheyenne* (Oklahoma) *Star*, 1990.
A long poem with a description of the Cheyennes who lived in the Hammon, Oklahoma, vicinity.

———. *One Hundred and One Schools Remembered*. Np., nd.
    A detailed book on all facets of Roger Mills County schools with histories of some.

Crane, Glena Belle. *Glen Crane's Record of Roger Mills County, Oklahoma Cemeteries and More*. Oklahoma City: Southwestern Stationery and Bank Supply, 1996.
    Perceptions of some of the first Anglo-Europeans to visit western Oklahoma by way of the Canadian River Valley and its tributaries: Stephen H. Long, Josiah Gregg, J. W. Abert, and Randolph Marcy.

Creel, Von Russell. "Socialists in the House: The Oklahoma Experience." *The Chronicles of Oklahoma* 70 (Summer, 1992):144–183; (Fall, 1992):258–301.
    Western Oklahoma counties elected five Socialists to the state legislature of 1915–1916. They influenced reform measures such as prohibition, regulation of corporations, poll taxes, and leasing state lands to tenant farmers.

Curtis, Edward S. *The North American Indian*, vol. 6 (1911), vol. 19 (1930). New York: Johnson Reprint, 1970. [ed. Frederick W. Hodge. Norwood, Mass.: Plimpton Press, 1907–1930].
    Curtis interviewed the Northern Cheyennes in 1911 and the Southern Cheyennes in 1930, focusing on nineteenth-century life. Includes a sketch of subsistence activity, ethnology, political organization, ceremonies, and origin stories of the Wichitas; a sketch of the Comanches; and briefer sketches of Caddos, Kiowas, Apaches, Choctaws, and Chickasaws.

"Custer's Oklahoma Fight." Unidentified newspaper clipping, 1904. "Wars—Battle of the Washita." Section X, Oklahoma Historical Society, Oklahoma City, Oklahoma.
    Description of the Washita Massacre as seen by Ben Clark.

"Custer's Washita Fight." *New York Sun*, May 14, 1899. Fred S. Barde Collection, Oklahoma Historical Society, Oklahoma City, Oklahoma.
    Description of the Washita Massacre as seen by Ben Clark.

Dale, Edward Everett. *Cow Country*. Norman: University of Oklahoma Press, 1942, 1965 edition.
    This book describes the growth of the range cattle industry and details the techniques of driving cattle up the western trails to Kansas railheads. Dale was a cowboy before he earned his doctorate in history.

———. *Ranching on the Cheyenne-Arapaho Reservation, 1880–1885*. Np., nd. Oklahoma Historical Society, Oklahoma City, Oklahoma.
    This is the classic study of ranching on the Cheyenne-Arapaho Reservation, the creation of the Cheyenne-Arapaho Live Stock Association, and federal policy leading to the expulsion of the ranchers.

Davis, Clara King. *The Winds of Change on Croton Creek*. Stillwater, Okla.: New Forums Press, 1997.
An account of the King family during a century on the Bar Z Ranch on Croton Creek in Roger Mills County.

Debo, Angie. *The Rise and Fall of the Choctaw Republic*. Norman: University of Oklahoma Press, 1934.
Classic history of the Choctaws from early contact to the dissolution of the Choctaw government in Indian Territory.

———. *And Still the Waters Run*. Princeton: Princeton University Press, 1940.
Debo's classic account of the dissolution of the Chickasaw and Choctaw governments and the loss of their lands.

Derrick, W. Edwin. "Fort Reno: Defender of the Southern Plains." In *Early Military Forts and Posts in Oklahoma*, ed. Odie B. Faulk, Kenny A. Franks, and Paul A. Lambert. Oklahoma City: Oklahoma Historical Society, 1978.
An overview of Fort Reno's history from founding through the end of its military use in 1948.

Dobak, William A. "Fort Riley's Black Soldiers and the Army's Changing Role in the West, 1867–1885." *Kansas History* 22 (Fall, 1999): 214–227.
The "buffalo soldiers" of the Ninth and Tenth Cavalry regiments, based at Fort Riley, Kansas, first protected railroad construction crews from Indian attack and then were reassigned to keep "boomers" out of Indian lands in western Oklahoma.

Dorsey, George A. *The Arapaho Sun Dance: The Ceremony of the Offerings Lodge*. Field Columbian Museum Publication 75, Anthropological Series, vol. 4, 1903.
A description of the Southern Arapaho Sun Dance.

———. *The Cheyenne: The Sun Dance. Field Columbian Museum Publication* 103, Anthropological Series, vol. 9, no. 2, 1905.
A description of the Southern Cheyenne Sun Dance.

———. *The Mythology of the Wichita*. Carnegie Institution of Washington 21, 1904. Norman: University of Oklahoma Press, 1995 edition.
A collection of origin stories obtained in 1903 from eight Tawakoni, four Waco, seven Wichita elders. Many of the stories came from Tawakoni Jim, the head chief. The interpreter was Burgess Hunt. The monograph also has an introductory chapter with information on social organization, religion, and technology.

———. *Traditions of the Caddo*. New York: AMS [1905].
A collection of stories of creation and the trickster.

Drass, Richard R. "The Southern Plains Villagers." In *Archaeology on the Great Plains*, ed. W. Raymond Wood. Lawrence: University Press of Kansas, 1998.

An overview of archaeological research on the Southern Plains, the article identifies sites linked to the Wichitas.

Drass, Richard R., and Timothy G. Baugh. "The Wheeler Phase and Cultural Continuity in the Southern Plains." *Plains Anthropologist* 42 (no. 160, 1997):183–204.
Plains Caddoans, probably related to the Wichita groups of north-central Oklahoma and Kansas, lived in Custer and Washita counties about A.D. 1400–1700.

Ediger, Theodore A., and Vinnie Hoffman. "Some Reminiscences of the Battle of the Washita." *The Chronicles of Oklahoma* 33 (Summer, 1955):137–141.
The reminiscences of Moving Behind and Wolf Belly Woman.

Eggan, Fred. "The Cheyenne and Arapaho Kinship System" in *Social Anthropology of North American Tribes*. Chicago: University of Chicago, 1955.
Eggan compared Cheyenne and Arapaho kinship terminology and behavior. He interviewed Cheyennes and Arapahos in Oklahoma in 1933.

Flynn, Peggy. "Analysis of Test Excavations at the Zimms Site (34RM72), Western Oklahoma." *Plains Anthropologist* 31 (no. 114, pt.2, 1986): 129–140.
The Zimms site in Roger Mills County is a square semisubterranean wattle and daub structure more similar to sites along the lower Washita River than sites in the Texas Panhandle.

Foreman, Grant. *Advancing the Frontier, 1830–1860*. Norman: University of Oklahoma Press, 1933.
A classic resource for the history of Indian Territory during this period.

———. "Early Trails through Oklahoma." *The Chronicles of Oklahoma* 3 (Summer, 1925):99–119.
This article briefly describes the early routes Anglo-Americans followed through the Indian Territory in the pre–Civil War period.

———. *The Five Civilized Tribes: Cherokee, Chickasaw, Choctaw, Creek, Seminole*. Norman: University of Oklahoma Press, 1934, 1970 edition.
Covers the history of the Chickasaws and Choctaws between Indian Territory settlement and the Civil War.

———. *Indians and Pioneers: The Story of the American Southwest Before 1830*. Norman: University of Oklahoma Press, 1936.
Foreman covers the Oklahoma frontier from 1541 through the beginning of the removal of the eastern Indians. Included are Spanish, French, and early Anglo-American exploration and trade along the Canadian River Valley.

————. *Marcy and the Gold Seekers: The Journal of Capt. R. B. Marcy with an Account of the Gold Rush Over the Southern Route*. Norman: University of Oklahoma Press, 1939.
This book details the extensive travel east to west along the California Road, emphasizing the Gold Rush period. Footnotes contain complete primary documents and newspaper sources from early travelers on the divide between the Canadian and Washita rivers.

Foreman, Grant, ed. "Survey of a Wagon Road from Fort Smith to the Colorado River." *The Chronicles of Oklahoma* 12 (Spring, 1934): 74–96.
Edward F. Beale surveyed a possible route for the continental railroad from Fort Smith to the Antelope Hills in the winter of 1858. He and F. E. Engle concluded that the California Road along the Canadian and Washita rivers offered the best topography and that a railroad could be built along it for $9,311,900.

Foster, Morris W. *Being Comanche: A Social History of an American Indian Community*. Tucson: University of Arizona, 1991.
General overview of Comanche social organization from the time of early contact with Europeans to the present.

Foster, Morris W., and Martha McCollough. "Plains Apache." In *Handbook of North American Indians: Plains*, Vol. 13, ed. Raymond J. DeMallie. Gen. ed., William C. Sturtevant. Washington D.C.: Smithsonian Institution, 2001.
An overview of history and sociocultural organization of Plains Apaches.

Fowler, Arlen L. *The Black Infantry in the West, 1869–1891*. Norman: University of Oklahoma Press, 1996.
Information on the service of the Twenty-fourth Infantry stationed at Fort Supply.

Fowler, Loretta. *The Arapaho*. New York: Chelsea House Publishers, 1989.
A comprehensive and comparative culture history of the Northern and Southern Arapahos written for the general reader.

————. *Arapahoe Politics, 1851–1968: Symbols in Crises of Authority*. Lincoln: University of Nebraska, 1982.
Based on primary sources and field observations, this study of the Northern Arapahos also includes material on the Southern Arapahos before 1851.

————. *Draft Report, Ethnographic Overview (Phase III) for Washita Battlefield National Historical Site*. Cooperative Agreement No. 143CA 125098002 (Modification 4). National Park Service, March 27, 2003.
A study of the association of Indian tribes other than the Cheyennes with Washita Battlefield National Historic Site.

———. *Final Report, Ethnographic Overview (Phase II) for Washita Battlefield National Historic Site.* Cooperative Agreement No. 143CA 125098002 (Modification 3) National Park Service, 2001.
A study of the Cheyenne Indians and their association with the site of the Washita Massacre.

———. *Shared Symbols, Contested Meanings: Gros Ventre Culture and History, 1778–1984.* Ithaca: Cornell University Press, 1987.
Based on primary sources, this is a study of the Gros Ventre, including early relations between the Arapaho divisions prior to reservation settlement.

———. *Tribal Sovereignty and the Historical Imagination: Cheyenne-Arapaho Politics.* Lincoln: University of Nebraska, 2002.
A detailed study based on primary sources and field observations of Cheyenne and Arapaho government and politics from 1869 to 1999.

Gates, Gladys Esther. "The Wichita Indians from 1859 to 1868." Master's thesis, University of Oklahoma, 1926.
Based largely on *Annual Reports of the Commissioner of Indian Affairs*, this thesis focuses on the Wichitas during the Civil War.

Gibson, Arrell Morgan. *The American Indian: Prehistory to the Present.* Norman: University of Oklahoma Press, 1980.
This standard general history of American Indians discusses federal policies that affected military conquest and settlement of western Oklahoma.

———. *The Chickasaws.* Norman: University of Oklahoma Press, 1971.
This is the standard history of the Chickasaws up to 1907.

———. *Oklahoma: A History of Five Centuries.* Norman: University of Oklahoma Press, 1965, 1981 edition.
This is the standard history of Oklahoma and is written for the student.

Gildaym, John P., and Mark H. Salt, eds. *Oklahoma History South of the Canadian.* Vol. 1. Chicago: S. J. Clarke Publishing Company, 1925.
A historical and biographical collection on southwestern Oklahoma.

Gladwin, Thomas. "Comanche Kin Behavior." *American Anthropologist*, New Series 50 (1948):73–94.
Description of kinship terminology and behavior.

Goetzmann, William H. *Army Exploration in the American West, 1803–1863.* New Haven, Conn.: Yale University Press, 1959.
Accounts of explorations sponsored by the U.S. War Department from the Louisiana Purchase to the Civil War are summarized and placed in context. Reprinted maps are included.

Greene, Jerome A. *Historic Resource Study. Washita Battlefield National Historic Site, Oklahoma.* Denver: [National Park Service], 2001.
A historical study of the U.S. Army and the Southern Cheyennes 1867–1869.

"Gregg's Commerce of the Prairies." *Early Western Travels, 1748–1846. A Series of Annotated Reprints . . . of Social and Economic Conditions in the Middle and Far West, during the Period of Early American Settlement*, ed. Reuben Gold Thwaites. Cleveland: Arthur H. Clark, 1907.
A classic account of travel to Santa Fe and return through the Indian Territory.

Hagan, William T. *Quanah Parker, Comanche Chief*. Norman: University of Oklahoma Press, 1993.
Life history of an important Kwahadi leader.

———. *United States-Comanche Relations: The Reservation Years*. New Haven: Yale University Press, 1976.
Good history of Comanche relations with the United States from the Treaty of Medicine Lodge Creek through the early reservation days when cattle leasing influenced reservation politics. The author also discusses the Jerome Agreement and the allotment process and provides material on Quanah Parker.

Hale, Douglas. *The Germans from Russia in Oklahoma*. Norman: University of Oklahoma Press, 1980.
An account of the settlement and history of German-Russian immigrants in Oklahoma, particularly in Custer and Washita counties.

Hale, Duane K., and Arrell M. Gibson. *The Chickasaw*. New York: Chelsea House, 1991.
An overview of history and sociocultural organization from prior to European contact to the present-day, this book is written for a general audience.

Haley, J. Evetts. *Charles Goodnight: Cowman and Plainsman*. Norman: University of Oklahoma, 1936.
This account of the life of a noted Texas rancher also contains a chapter on the *comancheros* and New Mexican inhabitants of the Texas Panhandle.

Hammond, George P., and Agapito Rey, eds. *Don Juan De Onate: Colonizer of New Mexico, 1595–1628*. Coronado Cuarto Centennial Publications, 1540–1940, Vol. 6. N.p.: University of New Mexico, 1953.
Translations of original documents associated with one of the earliest Spanish explorers of western Oklahoma. "Expedition to the North, 1601" described the Canadian River Valley of the Texas Panhandle, buffalo, flora and fauna, and the Plains Apaches that inhabited this area.

Hancock, Richard H. "William Box Hancock, Trail Driver and Cattleman." *The Chronicles of Oklahoma* 76 (Winter, 1998):356– 373.
This description of herding cattle up the Great Western Cattle Trail through Roger Mills County from 1879 to 1884 is based on W. B. Hancock's manuscript reminiscences.

Hanson, Jeffrey R. "The Late High Plains Hunters." In *Archaeology on the Great Plains*, ed. W. Raymond Wood. Lawrence: University Press of Kansas, 1998.
Discusses several Plains Apache groups' association with the Dismal River archaeological sites.

Harper, Elizabeth Ann. "The Taovayas Indians in Frontier Trade and Diplomacy, 1779–1835." *Panhandle-Plains Historical Review* 23 (1953): 1–32.
Excellent discussion on relations between Europeans and the Taovaya division of the Wichitas based on primary sources.

Harrel, Melvin. "The History of Bar X Lands." *The Chronicles of Oklahoma* 29 (Spring 1951):70–78.
Gives an overview of cattle ranching in Roger Mills County and vicinity from 1876 through 1885. Includes a sketch map and very brief descriptions of earlier exploration.

———. "'My Life in the Indian Territory of Oklahoma': The Story of Augusta Corson Metcalf." *The Chronicles of Oklahoma* 33 (Spring, 1955):49–62.
Artist Augusta Metcalfe's remembrances of her life in pioneer Day County and Roger Mills County.

Harris, La Donna. *A Comanche Life*. ed. H. Henrietta Stockel. Lincoln: University of Nebraska Press, 2000.
Autobiography of a prominent leader who played an important role in Oklahoma during the War on Poverty era of the 1960s.

Heeney, Marjorie Savage. "Cheyenne Memories." *Cheyenne* (Oklahoma) *Star*, April 19, 1990.
A description of the Cheyenne Indians who lived along Whiteshield Creek near Hammon, Oklahoma.

Henslick, Harry E. "Abraham Jefferson Seay: Governor of Oklahoma Territory, 1892–1893." *The Chronicles of Oklahoma* 53 (Spring, 1975): 28–45.
Describes the work of the territorial governor who oversaw the opening of the Cheyenne and Arapaho Reservation and the creation of the six new western counties.

Hilger, M. Inez. *Arapaho Child Life and its Cultural Background*. Smithsonian Institution, Bureau of American Ethnology, Bulletin 148, 1952.
Sister Hilger, working under the auspices of the Bureau of American Ethnology, made a detailed study of childhood, adolescence, and gender roles among Northern and Southern Arapahos. She interviewed elderly Southern Arapahos in 1935 and 1941.

———. "Notes on Cheyenne Child Life." *American Anthropologist* 48 (1946):60–69.
Hilger made a brief comparative study of Cheyenne customs surrounding infancy and childhood.

Hillegass, Margaret Dietzel. "Rodolphe Petter: A 'Called' Linguist." *Mennonite Life* 3 (no. 2, 1982):4–7.
Describes the work of Swiss Mennonite missionary Rodolphe Petter from 1892 to 1947, during which he developed a grammar and dictionary of the Cheyenne language.

Hodge, Pat. "The History of Hammon and the Red Moon School." *The Chronicles of Oklahoma* 44 (Summer, 1966):130–139.
The Roger Mills County town of Hammon took its name from James and Ida Hammon, who established the Red Moon Boarding School, the most modern school in western Oklahoma, in 1897.

———. "Red Moon Boarding School." *The Cheyenne* (Oklahoma) *Star*, April 19, 1990.
A description of Red Moon Boarding School at Hammon, Oklahoma.

Hoebel, E. Adamson. "On Cheyenne Sociopolitical Organization." *Plains Anthropologist* 25 (1980):161–169.
Based on interviews, this article is a reconstruction of the organization and activity of chiefs and military societies.

———. *Political Organization and Law-Ways of the Comanche Indians. Memoirs of the American Anthropological Association* 54, 1940.
A study of Comanche dispute settlement based on interviews done in 1933.

Hofman, Jack L. "The Plains Villages: The Custer Phase." *Prehistory of Oklahoma*, ed. R. E. Bell. Orlando: Academic Press, 1984.
Somewhat dated article written for specialists, it discusses the Dismal River archaeological sites and why Plains Apaches are related to these sites.

Hofsommer, Donovan L. "Oklahoma Railroad Maintenance Authority: An Example of Rural Pressure Group Politics." *Journal of the West* 13 (October, 1974):108–116.
Demonstrates the importance of railroads to farmers, ranchers, businessmen, and legislators in western Oklahoma by examining attempts to prevent the nearly bankrupt Missouri, Kansas and Texas Railroad from abandoning branch lines.

———. "What is the Future for Railroad Branch Lines in Rural Areas?" *The Chronicles of Oklahoma* 56 (Winter, 1978):393–408.
The Interstate Commerce Commission permitted three branch lines in western Oklahoma to be abandoned in 1973 in spite of protests by grain elevator operators and wheat farmers that continued service was an economic necessity.

Hoig, Stan. *The Battle of the Washita: The Sheridan-Custer Indian Campaign of 1867–69*. Garden City: Doubleday, 1976.
A detailed history of the Washita fight, including information about the participation of several tribes.

———. *Tribal Wars of the Southern Plains*. Norman: University of Oklahoma Press, 1993.
   Useful as an overview of Southern Plains warfare from the advent of the horse to the 1870s.

Holding, Vera. "A Heritage to Share." *The Chronicles of Oklahoma* 42 (Spring, 1964):2–6.
   Ida Cooke narrated her family's experience traveling to Custer County, Oklahoma, following the opening of the Cheyenne and Arapaho Reservation in 1892. She describes living in a sod house, attending school in a dugout, and moving into a half-dugout with her new husband.

Hollon, W. Eugene. *Beyond the Cross Timbers: The Travels of Randolph B. Marcy, 1812–1887*. Norman: University of Oklahoma Press, 1955.
   This biography details the expeditions through the Canadian River Valley of one of the primary explorers of the southwest in the mid-nineteenth century.

Horr, David Agee, ed. *Kiowa-Comanche Indians: Transcript of Hearings of the Kiowa, Comanche, and Apache Tribes of Indians vs. The United States of America*, 2 vols. *American Indian Ethnohistory*. Plains, N.Y.: Garland, 1974.
   Testimony of elderly Indians who were present at the Jerome Commission council concerning allotment of the reservation.

Hughes, J. Patrick. "Forts and Camps in Oklahoma Before the Civil War." In *Early Military Forts and Posts in Oklahoma*, ed. Odie B. Faulk, Kenny A. Franks, and Paul F. Lambert. Oklahoma City: Oklahoma Historical Society, 1978, 39–53.
   An overview of the military presence in pre–Civil War Oklahoma, including Camp Radziminski and Fort Cobb in western Oklahoma.

Hyde, George E. *The Life of George Bent, Written from his Letters*, ed. Savoie Lottinville. Norman: University of Oklahoma Press, 1968.
   Bent was the son of the trader William Bent and his Cheyenne wife. He married Black Kettle's niece and wrote letters about his experiences living with the Cheyennes.

Jablow, Joseph. *The Cheyenne in Plains Indian Trade Relations, 1795–1840. American Ethnological Society Monograph* 19, 1951.
   Based on primary sources, this study considers the ways that participation in trade with Europeans and Americans influenced Cheyenne life.

James, Edwin. "S. H. Long's Expedition." *Early Western Travels, 1748–1846*, ed. Reuben Gold Thwaites, Vol. 16. Cleveland: Arthur H. Clark Company, 1905.
   A first-person account of an 1820 federal survey of the upper Washita River Valley through Roger Mills County.

James, Louise Boyd. *Below Devil's Gap: The Story of Woodward County*. Perkins, Okla.: Evans Publications, 1984.

A good, competent local history of lands near Fort Supply and adjacent to the Cheyenne and Arapaho Reservation.

———. "Jujubes, Grapes, and Grass: The USDA Research Station at Woodward, 1913–1987." *The Chronicles of Oklahoma* 65 (Winter, 1987):354–379.
Describes the efforts of Superintendent Ellery "Frank" Chilcott to introduce new crops, grasses, and livestock breeds to help diversify the western Oklahoma economy.

John, Elizabeth A. H. "An Earlier Chapter of Kiowa History." *New Mexico Historical Review* 60 (1985):379–397.
Based on primary sources, identifies Kiowa interactions with the Spanish in New Mexico in the early and late eighteenth century.

———. "Nurturing the Peace." *New Mexico Historical Review* 59 (1984): 345–369.
Discusses efforts of Comanche leaders to establish trading relations and unify Comanche divisions on the New Mexico and Texas frontiers. Based on primary sources.

———. "Portraits of a Wichita Village, 1808." *The Chronicles of Oklahoma* 60 (Winter, 1982):412–437.
Based on primary sources, the article gives a description of lifeways in a Taovaya village.

———. *Storms Brewed in Other Men's Worlds: The Confrontation of Indians, Spanish, and French in the Southwest.* College Station: Texas A. and M. University, 1975.
Good overview of intertribal and European-Indian relations on the Southern Plains from contact to the early eighteenth century.

Johnson, Bobby H. "Booster Attitudes of Some Newspapers in Oklahoma Territory— 'The Land of the Fair God.'" *The Chronicles of Oklahoma* 43 (Fall, 1965):242–262.
Examines the role of newspapers in the Cheyenne and Arapaho Reservation towns of El Reno, Watonga, Kingfisher, and Arapaho in town promotion.

Jones, David E. *Sanapia: Comanche Medicine Woman.* New York: Holt, Rinehart and Winston, 1972.
A good study of the life of a Northern Comanche woman and her training and role as a doctor. Includes detailed information on the use of wild plants.

Jones, Douglas C. *The Treaty of Medicine Lodge: The Story of the Great Treaty Council as Told by Eyewitnesses.* Norman: University of Oklahoma Press, 1966.
A description of events leading up to and during the treaty council at Medicine Lodge Creek in 1867.

Jordan, Julia Anne. "Ethnobotany of the Kiowa-Apache." Master's thesis, University of Oklahoma, 1965.

This is an excellent study of plant use by the Apaches at the time of this study, 1963–1964.

———. "Comanche." *Handbook of North American Indians: Plains*, Vol.13, ed. Raymond J. DeMallie. Gen. ed. William C. Sturtevant. Washington, D.C.: Smithsonian Institution, 2001.
Overview of Comanche history and sociocultural organization; includes a section on sources.

Kavanagh, Thomas W. *Comanche Political History: An Ethnohistorical Perspective, 1706–1875*. Lincoln: University of Nebraska Press, 1996.
A comprehensive ethnohistorical study of the Comanche people, with discussion of the significance of the 1858 Battle of Antelope Hills (Little Robe Creek).

Kenner, Charles L. *A History of New Mexican-Plains Indian Relations*. Norman: University of Oklahoma Press, 1969.
Covers the Spanish and New Mexican presence on the Southern Plains from 1598 to 1880 as hunters, traders, and ranchers. Of particular interest are the *ciboleros* and *comancheros* who visited western Oklahoma to hunt and trade with the Indians.

———. *Buffalo Soldiers and Officers of the Ninth Cavalry, 1867–1898: Black and White Together*. Norman: University of Oklahoma Press, 1999.
A history of one of the two black cavalry regiments important in the pacification and settlement of the Southern Plains.

Kenner, Charles LeRoy. "New Mexican Penetration of the Texas Panhandle during the Nineteenth Century." Master's thesis, Panhandle A. and M. College, Goodwell, Oklahoma, 1954.
The foundation study for the work above. This version focuses on the New Mexican *ciboleros, comancheros,* and *pastores* in the Texas Panhandle in the 1800s.

Kroeber, Alfred L. *The Arapaho*. Lincoln: University of Nebraska, 1983.
Using interviews with both Northern and Southern Arapahos, Kroeber provides an overview of nineteenth-century life, focusing on the age-graded lodges and the Sun Dance.

———. "Arapaho Dialects." In *Publications in American Archaeology and Ethnology* 12 (1916):3.
This study includes information on the early divisions of the Arapahos in the eighteenth century.

Kroeker, Marvin E. "'Die Stillen im Lande': Mennonites in the Oklahoma Land Rushes." *The Chronicles of Oklahoma* 67 (Spring, 1989):76–97.
Mennonites settled in the Cheyenne and Arapaho Reservation as early as 1880 and participated in each of the land runs in the 1890s. By 1907 there were forty-four Mennonite and Amish communities, mostly in Blaine, Custer, and Washita counties.

La Barre, Weston. "Kiowa Folk Sciences." *Journal of American Folklore* 60 (1947):105–114.

An examination of Kiowa ethnobiology, including the Kiowas' knowledge of plants.

La Vere, David. *Contrary Neighbors: Southern Plains and Removed Indians in Indian Territory*. Norman: University of Oklahoma Press, 2000.
The book focuses on differences and relationships between the Five Civilized Tribes (including Choctaws and Chickasaws) and the Plains and other Indians in Indian Territory during the nineteenth century.

La Vere, David, and Katia Campbell, eds. "An Expedition to the Kichai: The Journal of Francois Grappe, September 24, 1783." *Southwestern Historical Quarterly* 98 (Spring, 1994):59–78.
The journal records a trip from Natchitoches in Spanish Louisiana to trade in a Kichai village. There is information of lifeways and political behavior.

Lassiter, Luke E. *The Power of Kiowa Song: A Collaborative Ethnography*. Tucson: University of Arizona, 1998.
Anthropological study of Kiowa singing, written as a dialogue between the anthropologist and the singers.

Lassiter, Luke Eric, Clyde Ellis, and Ralph Kotay. *The Jesus Road: Kiowas, Christianity, and Indian Hymns*. Lincoln: University of Nebraska, 2002.
Study of the indigenization of Christianity based on collaborative research by an anthropologist, a historian, and a Kiowa singer.

Leckie, William H. *The Military Conquest of the Southern Plains*. Norman: University of Oklahoma Press, 1963.
A standard work for the Red River War.

Le Van, Sandra W. "The Quaker Agents at Darlington." *The Chronicles of Oklahoma* 51 (Spring, 1973):92–99.
A description of the lives of the Quaker Indian agents assigned to the Cheyenne Indians from 1868 to1886.

Levy, Jerrold E. "After Custer: Kiowa Political and Social Organization from the Reservation Period to the Present." Doctoral dissertation, University of Chicago, 1959.
Levy did fieldwork in 1957–1958. He describes social and political activity at that time and establishes links between life in the early reservation time and the 1950s, including how formal social ranking of families affected and was affected by reservation politics. He views the Washita Massacre as the beginning of the military conquest of the Kiowas.

———. "Kiowa." *Handbook of North American Indians: Plains*, Vol. 13, ed. Raymond J. DeMallie. Gen. ed. William C. Sturtevant. Washington DC: Smithsonian Institution, 2001.
An overview of Kiowa history and sociocultural organization; includes a section on sources.

Linscheid, Ruth C. *Red Moon*. Newton, Kan.: Union Printing, 1973.
Brief history of the Red Moon band of Cheyennes, the mission school, and settlement located near them, based on the experiences of her father, G. A. Linscheid.

Llewellyn, Karl N., and Adamson Hoebel. *The Cheyenne Way: Conflict and Case Law in Primitive Jurisprudence*. Norman: University of Oklahoma Press, 1941.
Based on interviews, this study focuses on dispute settlement during the nineteenth century.

Loomis, Noel M., and Abraham P. Nasatir. *Pedro Vial and the Roads to Santa Fe*. Norman: University of Oklahoma Press, 1967.
A description of the contributions of a pathfinder in the Southern Plains during the Spanish control of Louisiana.

Mahnken, Norbert R. "The Cheyenne Short Line: Oklahoma's 'Do It Yourself' Railroad." *The Chronicles of Oklahoma* 62 (Summer, 1984): 120–133.
Cheyenne, Oklahoma, residents built their own seven-mile railroad to connect with the Clinton and Oklahoma Western Railway line in 1916 to provide transportation for their own agricultural produce and to keep Cheyenne as the seat of Roger Mills County.

Marriott, Alice. *The Ten Grandmothers*. Norman: University of Oklahoma Press, 1945, 1989 edition.
Reconstruction of life in the nineteenth and early twentieth centuries based on oral history. Marriott did fieldwork in 1935–1944. Among the stories are the seizure of Sitting Bear, White Bear, and Big Tree and the captivity of the hostile Kiowas at Fort Sill.

Martin, Charles E. "'A Good One is a Dead One': The Combat Soldiers' View of Vietnam and the Indian Wars." *Kentucky Folklore Record* 26 (nos. 3-4, 1980):114–132.
Compares combat soldiers' attitudes at the 1868 Washita Massacre to those of American soldiers in the 1968 My Lai Massacre in Vietnam.

Mathews, John Joseph. *The Osages: Children of the Middle Waters*. Norman: University of Oklahoma Press, 1961.
This is a history of the Osages by an Osage writer.

Mayhall, Mildred P. *The Kiowas*. Norman: University of Oklahoma Press, 1962.
A standard history of the Kiowas.

McAllister, J. Gilbert. "Kiowa-Apache Social Organization." In *Social Anthropology of North American Tribes*, ed. Fred Eggan. Chicago: University of Chicago, 1955, second edition.
This is a detailed study of kinship terminology and behavior and the life cycle.

———. "Daveko: Kiowa-Apache Medicine Man." *Texas Memorial Museum* 17 (1970): 21–61.

In 1933–1934 McAllister collected information on the life of one of the most prominent doctors among the Apaches. Daveko was active in the late nineteenth century, after obtaining his powers on a vision quest. There is also information on Apache society.

McKinney, Gary. "Oklahoma Ghost Town Journalism." *The Chronicles of Oklahoma* 46 (Winter, 1968):387–408.
A description of *The Day County Tribune, The Day County Progress,* and *The Canadian Valley Echo* published at Grand before the demise of Day County in 1907. The *Progress* and *Echo* moved to Cheyenne, where the latter continued under a new name.

Meadows, William C. *Kiowa, Apache, and Comanche Military Societies: Enduring Veterans, 1800 to the Present.* Austin: University of Texas, 1999.
Detailed comparative study of the history of military societies and their transformations in social form and meaning.

Meredith, Howard. *Dancing on Common Ground: Tribal Cultures and Alliances on the Southern Plains.* Lawrence: University Press of Kansas, 1995.
General history of Caddos, Wichitas, Kiowas, Comanches, and Apaches. The book draws on interviews and places the tribal histories and interactions in the context of Plains ecology. It includes contemporary times.

———. "Whirlwind: A Study of Church-State Relationships." *Historical Magazine of the Protestant Episcopal Church* 43 (no. 4, 1974):297–304.
Describes the conflict between the federal government and the Episcopal bishop of Oklahoma over the closing of Whirlwind Day School and the transfer of the Cheyenne and Arapaho students to the agency boarding school.

Michelson, Truman. "Narrative of an Arapaho Woman." *American Anthropologist* 35 (1933):4.
Michelson recorded this biography of an elderly woman.

———. "The Narrative of a Southern Cheyenne Woman." *Smithsonian Miscellaneous Collections* 85, no. 5 (1932):1–13.
Michelson recorded a brief autobiography of an elderly woman.

Mitchell, Michael Dan. "Acculturation Problems among the Plains Tribes of the Governmental Agencies in Western Indian Territory." *The Chronicles of Oklahoma* 44 (Winter, 1966):281–289.
Describes Quaker missionaries among the western Indian Territory tribes, as well as the influence of "border whites." Quakers established a school among the Cheyennes and Arapahos in 1871.

Mooney, James. *Calendar History of the Kiowa Indians.* Washington D.C.: Smithsonian Institution, 1898.
Mooney did fieldwork in the 1890s. The book sketches Apache history and gives detailed information on Kiowa history and socio-

cultural organization. Mooney describes and provides ethnographic information on two pictorial histories (1832–1892) by Kiowas.

———. "Calendar History of the Kiowa." *Seventeenth Annual Report of the Bureau of American Ethnology, 1895–1896*, Vol. 17, pt. 1. Washington, D.C.: Government Printing Office, 1898.
Same as above.

———. The Cheyenne Indians. *American Anthropological Association Memoirs* 1 (1907):357–442.
Mooney provides an overview of Cheyenne life in the nineteenth century.

———. *The Ghost-Dance Religion and the Sioux Outbreak of 1890. Annual Report of the Bureau of American Ethnology* 14 (1896):641–1110.
Mooney visited the Southern Cheyennes and Arapahos in 1891 and recorded aspects of their history as well as Ghost Dance activity.

Moore, John H. *The Cheyenne.* Cambridge, Mass.: Blackwell Publishers, 1966.
A general overview of Cheyenne culture and history written for the general reader. It is particularly useful for its discussion of cosmology and ceremonies.

———. *The Cheyenne Nation: A Social and Demographic History.* Lincoln: University of Nebraska, 1987.
A history of Cheyenne tribal divisions and their change over time.

Moore, Michael C. "Western Oklahoma Settlement Patterns: A Study of the Quartermaster Creek Watershed in Roger Mills and Custer Counties." *Plains Anthropologist* 31 (1986, part 2):97–110.
This survey showed intensive prehistoric occupation of the Quartermaster Creek watershed over the past 2,000 years in scattered camps and large permanent villages. Euro-American sites appeared in the late 1880s.

Morris, John W., Charles R. Goins, and Edwin C. McReynolds. *Historical Atlas of Oklahoma.* Norman: University of Oklahoma Press, third edition, 1986.
This useful collection of maps for Oklahoma history contains information on the exploration and transportation routes through western Oklahoma.

Neighbors, Kenneth. "Jose Maria: Anadarko Chief." *The Chronicles of Oklahoma* 44 (Fall, 1966):254–274.
A biography that draws on primary sources and an interview with the great-granddaughter of Jose Maria.

Newcomb, William N. *The Indians of Texas from Prehistoric to Modern Times.* Austin: University of Texas, 1961.
A general survey.

———. *The People Called Wichita.* Phoenix: Indian Tribal Series, 1976.
An overview of Wichita history written for a general audience.

———. "Wichita." In *Handbook of North American Indians: Plains*, 2 vols, ed. Raymond J. DeMallie. Gen. ed. William C. Sturtevant. Washington, D.C.: Smithsonian Institution, 2001.
Brief sketch of history, social organization, and belief system from early contact to modern times. Contains a discussion of the origin of band, division, and tribal names.

Newkumet, Vynola Beaver, and Howard Meredith. *Hasinai: A Traditional History of the Caddo Confederacy*. College Station: Texas A&M University Press, c.1988.
This collaboration between a historian and tribal member explains how stories of Caddo origins and historical activities are integrated into ceremonial life oriented to agriculture, hunting, and successful adaptation.

Noyes, Stanley. *Los Comanches: The Horse People, 1751–1845*. Albuquerque: University of New Mexico Press, 1993.
Readable, general account of Comanche life and relations with other peoples on the Southern Plains.

Nye, W. S. *Carbine and Lance: The Story of Old Fort Sill*. Norman: University of Oklahoma Press, 1937, 1969 edition.
A classic work on the history of Fort Sill and western Oklahoma during the Plains Wars. Nye was an officer at the fort and collected information from many Indians who had fought during the Indian wars.

Nye, Wilbur S. *Plains Indian Raiders: The Final Phases of Warfare from the Arkansas to the Red River*. Norman: University of Oklahoma Press, 1968.
A companion work to *Carbine and Lance* but less specific to Fort Sill.

Ottaway, Harold N. "Cascorillo: Archaeological Fact or Romantic Fantasy?" *The Chronicles of Oklahoma* 49 (Spring, 1971):100–104.
Describes attempts of archaeologists to determine whether there is fact in a local legend concerning Mexican mining operations in Washita County. Based on an 1895 article in *The Herald-Sentinel* of Cloud Chief, Oklahoma Territory.

Parsons, Elsie Clew. "Notes on the Caddo." *Memoirs of the American Anthropological Association*, no. 57 (1941):5–76.
An excellent ethnographic study in 1921–1922 and 1927 of the Caddo community. A Caddo graduate of Carlisle assisted Parsons. The study includes government, genealogies, household composition, settlement patterns, kinship, naming, health, economy, religion (Ghost Dance and Peyote ritual), dances, and oral traditions. Parsons emphasized sociocultural persistence.

Petter, Rodolphe. "Cheyenne Indians: A Photo Essay." *Mennonite Life* 37 (no. 2, 1982):8–13.
Photographs taken by Mennonite missionary Rodolphe Petter in Oklahoma and Montana from 1892 to 1947.

Perttula, Timothy. "The Caddo Nation." In *Archaeological and Ethno-historic Perspectives*. Austin: University of Texas, 1992.
Discusses the historic period using primary sources and archaeological research.

Pioneer History of Shattuck, A. Shattuck, Okla.: n.p., 1970.
This centennial book is a collection of institutional and family histories of the white families living near Shattuck.

Powell, Peter John. *People of the Sacred Mountain: A History of the Northern Cheyenne Chiefs and Warrior Societies, 1830–1879*. 2 vols. San Francisco: Harper and Row, 1979.
Powell's account is based on published accounts and interviews with Northern and Southern Cheyennes in the 1970s.

Purdy, Virginia C., ed. "'Dust to Eat': A Document from the Dust Bowl." *The Chronicles of Oklahoma* 58 (Winter, 1980–81):440–454.
Farm wife Caroline Agnes Boa Henderson describes the farming conditions in Oklahoma that helped bring on the Dust Bowl, as well as the New Deal programs designed to relieve the problems.

Rathjen, Frederick W. *The Texas Panhandle Frontier*. M. K. Brown Range Life Series, no.12. Austin: University of Texas, 1973.
A historical/geographical study of the Texas Panhandle adjacent to Roger Mills County, Oklahoma. Included are a physiographical and historical study by period from Indian occupation through the Anglo-American settlement by 1880.

Reggio, Michael H. "Troubled Times: Homesteading in Short-Grass Country, 1892–1900." *The Chronicles of Oklahoma* 57 (Summer, 1979): 196–211.
Drought, lack of transportation for crops, fear of Indians, and terrible living conditions hindered the settlement of the Cheyenne-Arapaho lands until 1906 in spite of the low filing fee.

Richards, O. H. "Early Days in Day County." *The Chronicles of Oklahoma* 26 (Fall, 1948):313–324.
Reminiscences of a Day County pioneer rancher.

Richardson, Jane Hanks. *Law and Status of the Kiowa Indians*. New York: Monographs of the American Ethnological Society, 1940.
Reconstruction of Kiowa life in the nineteenth century based on fieldwork in 1935. The focus is on how leaders competed for followers, how social mobility worked, and how disputes were settled.

Richardson, Rupert Norval. *The Comanche Barrier to South Plains Settlement: A Century and a Half of Savage Resistance to the Advancing White Frontier*. Glendale, Calif.: Arthur H. Clark, 1933.
A classic work on the Comanche Indians through 1872, emphasizing their strong role against Spanish and Anglo-American colonization of Texas.

Richie, E. B., ed. "Copy of the Report of Colonel Samuel Cooper of an Inspection Trip to Indian Villages on the Upper Brazos in June 1851." *Southwestern Historical Quarterly* 42 (1939):327–333.
Cooper went with John Sibley to visit Caddo villages, including Jose Maria's. The report also has information on Wichitas, Delawares, and Comanches.

Roger Mills Minute: A History of Roger Mills County, 1912–1992. Cheyenne, Okla.: Security State Bank, n.d.
A brief history of Roger Mills County and surrounding towns.

Rollings, Willard H. *The Comanche*. New York: Chelsea House, 1989.
Written for a general audience, the book covers Comanche history from the eighteenth century to the 1980s.

———. *The Osage: An Ethnohistorical Study of Hegemony on the Prairie Plains*. Columbia: University of Missouri, 1992.
This study examines the "empire" Osages claimed from the Missouri River Valley to the Red River.

Savage, Ted R. "The Black Kettle Memorial Celebration." *Cheyenne* (Oklahoma) *Star*, April 19, 1990.
Reminiscences of the Savage family's participation in the 1930 celebration.

Savage, William W. "Monologues in Red and White: Contemporary Racial Attitudes in Two Southern Plains Communities." *Journal of Ethnic Studies* 2 (no. 3, 1974): 24–31.
Examines racial attitudes among whites and Indians in two similar western Oklahoma towns of 1500 population. Based on materials in the Doris Duke Oral History Project, University of Oklahoma.

Schmidt, Joel J. "'Until the Mothers Are Reached': Field Matrons on the Cheyenne and Arapaho Reservation." *The Chronicles of Oklahoma* 74 (Winter, 1996):436–445.
Field matrons from 1889 to 1924 tried to change traditional Indian ways but failed to persuade Indian women away from communal dwellings and camps. Field matrons often felt superior to Indian women and spoke of them in degrading terms.

Schmitt, Karl. "Wichita Death Customs." *The Chronicles of Oklahoma* 30 (Summer, 1952):200–206.
Information on social structure.

———. *Wichita Kinship, Past and Present*. Norman: University Book Exchange, 1952.
Kinship terminology and behavior before the reservation period and during contemporary times.

———. "Wichita-Kiowa Relations and the 1874 Outbreak." *The Chronicles of Oklahoma* 28 (Summer, 1950):154–160.
Good oral history and explanation of how key events shape contemporary attitudes.

Schofield, Donald F. "W. M. D. Lee, Indian Trader." *Panhandle-Plains Historical Review* 54 (1981):vii–viii, 1–113.
  Describes the partnership of William McDole Lee and Albert E. Reynolds as Fort Supply traders with a clientele among the soldiers, Cheyennes, Arapahos, and buffalo hunters from 1869 to 1878. After venturing into cattle ranching in the Texas Panhandle, they dissolved their partnership in 1881.

Schrems, Suzanne H. "Teaching School on the Western Frontier: Acceptable Occupation for Nineteenth Century Women." *Montana* 37 (Fall, 1987): 54–63.
  Although some women earned enough capital to establish homesteads, most found that this alternative role did not provide the independence they wanted because of rigid regulations governing their employment. Based on interviews of Oklahoma pioneers in the Indian-Pioneer Papers, University of Oklahoma.

Seger, John H. "Cheyenne Marriage Customs." *Journal of American Folklore* 11 (1896):298–301.
  Seger was agent at Colony Agency and wrote of his observations of the Cheyennes he knew.

———. *Early Days among the Cheyenne and Arapaho Indians*, ed. Stanley Vestal. Norman: University of Oklahoma Press, 1979.
  This narrative by John Seger describes conditions at the Cheyenne and Arapaho Agency in the nineteenth century.

Smith, F. Todd. *The Caddo Indians: Tribes at the Convergence of Empires, 1542–1854*. College Station: Texas A&M University Press, 1995.
  A history based on primary sources on the Caddo confederacy from the time of contact with Europeans to the time of their removal from Texas. Covers three Caddo confederacies.

———. *The Caddos, the Wichitas, and the United States, 1846–1901*. College Station: Texas A&M University Press, 1996.
  A history of U.S.-Indian relations, the book is based on primary sources and provides details of life on the reservation.

———. *The Wichita Indians: Traders of Texas and the Southern Plains, 1540–1845*. College Station: Texas A&M University Press, 2000.
  Based on primary sources, the book covers Wichita and Kitsai history from the time of contact with Europeans to the time of their removal from Texas to Indian Territory.

Shirley, Glenn. *Temple Houston: Lawyer with a Gun*. Norman: University of Oklahoma Press, 1980.
  Although lacking citations and anecdotal in approach, this biography describes Houston's life in the Texas Panhandle of the 1880s, ranching in the Panhandle, his move to Woodward, Oklahoma Territory in 1894, and his career as a lawyer in the Fifth Judicial District of Oklahoma Territory, which included Roger Mills and surrounding counties.

Steele, Annie Laurie. "A History of the Sandstone Creek Area Up-stream Flood Prevention Project." *The Chronicles of Oklahoma* 58 (Winter, 1965):432–442.
A brief history of the flood control project in the Washita River water shed. It became the national model.

Stout, Joseph A., Jr., ed. *Frontier Adventurers: American Exploration in Oklahoma*. The Oklahoma Series, vol. 4. Oklahoma City: Oklahoma Historical Society, 1976.
A collection of essays describes Anglo-American exploration of Oklahoma from 1806 to 1853. See specifically articles on Stephen H. Long, Josiah Gregg, and Randolph B. Marcy.

Swanton, John R. *The Indians of the Southeast United States. Bulletin of the Bureau of American Ethnology*, no. 137. Washington D.C.: Smithsonian Institution, 1946.
Short sketches of the tribes of the Southeast and a general description of economy, technology, and social and ceremonial life.

———. *Source Material on the History and Ethnology of the Caddo Indians*. Norman: University of Oklahoma Press, 1942, 1996 edition.
This work is based on French and Spanish primary sources from the seventeenth and eighteenth centuries.

Tatum, Lawrie. *Our Red Brothers and the Peace Policy of President Ulysses S. Grant*. Philadelphia: John C. Winston, 1899.
A first-person account of the work of Quaker missionaries among the Southern Plains tribes. Includes Brinton Darlington and John D. Miles, agents to the Cheyennes and Arapahos.

Taylor, Anna J. "Hispanic Settlement of the Texas Panhandle-Plains, 1876–1884." *Panhandle-Plains Historical Review* 70 (1997):36–58.
New Mexican *pastores* brought their housing, farming, ranching, and settlement patterns to the Texas Panhandle, leaving their mark on the land.

Taylor, Nat A. *A Brief History of Roger Mills County*. Np., 1947. Reprinted by the Roger Mills County Genealogical Society, 1997.
This chatty little book was written by an early settler, educator, and state legislator from his own experience in the first half of the twentieth century. Anecdotal in approach but well organized, it includes chapters on transportation, courts, county officers, social customs, businesses, and churches.

———. "The Old Bar X Ranch." *The Chronicles of Oklahoma* 49 (Spring, 1971):83–91.
Describes cattle ranching in the pre-settlement period of the Cheyenne-Arapaho Reservation, the Great Western Cattle Trail, and the 65,000–acre ranch near present Leedey from the 1870s to about 1900.

Tennant, H. S. "The Two Cattle Trails." *The Chronicles of Oklahoma* 14 (March, 1936):84–122.

A description of the Chisholm and Great Western cattle trails, based on letters and documents by pioneer cattlemen. Maps show the trails by section, range, and township.

Their Story: A Pioneer Days Album of the Blaine County Area. Oklahoma City: The Heritage Book Committee, 1977.
This local history includes articles on communities, schools, early settlers, Cheyenne and Arapaho residents, Indian/white relations, black residents, sports, and local culture as well as family articles.

Thetford, Francis. "Battle of the Washita Centennial, 1968." *The Chronicles of Oklahoma* 46 (Winter, 1968):358–361.
A description of the commemoration of the Washita Massacre and the reburial of Cheyenne remains at Cheyenne, Oklahoma.

Thiesen, John D. "Rodolphe Petter and General Conference Missions." *Mennonite Life* 40 (no. 3, 1985):4–10.
Although Rodolphe Petter devoted many years to working as a Mennonite missionary and linguist, he was unsympathetic toward Cheyenne culture.

Thoburn, Joseph. "A Campaign of the Texas Rangers Against Comanches." *Sturm's Oklahoma Magazine* 10 (July 1910):30–38.
An account of the Battle of Antelope Hills in 1858 based on documentary research and interviews of participants, among them the last surviving Texas Ranger officer. An accompanying map reproduced badly.

Thomas, A. B. "Spanish Exploration of Oklahoma 1599–1792." *The Chronicles of Oklahoma* 6 (June, 1928):186–213.
This discussion, based on the work of H. E. Bolton, covers Spanish and French exploration of the southwest region, focusing on Oklahoma. Maps are included.

Thomas, Alfred B. "An Eighteenth Century Comanche Document." *American Anthropologist* 31 (1929):289–298.
A report on Comanche/Apache relations, Comanche military societies, Comanche relations with New Mexico, and a list of Comanche chiefs.

Tower, Michael. "Traders along the Washita: A Short History of the Shirley Trading Company." *The Chronicles of Oklahoma* 65 (Spring, 1987):4–15.
William and John Shirley created a cattle ranch and trading center at Anadarko on the Washita River in 1854–1875 while trading with the Waco, Tonkawa, Anadarko, Tawakoni, Keechi, and Caddo Indians of the Wichita Agency.

Trenholm, Virginia Cole. *The Arapahos: Our People.* Norman: University of Oklahoma Press, 1970.
A history of the Arapahos up to the time of reservation settlement.

Truteau, Jean Baptiste. "Journal of Jean Baptiste Truteau among the Arikara Indians in 1795." *Missouri Historical Society Collections* 4 (1912).
Truteau was a fur trader who traveled up the Missouri River and obtained information about the native peoples of the Plains in 1795.

Thwaites, Reuben Gold, ed. *Early Western Travels, 1748–1846. A Series of Annotated Reprints . . . of Social and Economic Conditions in the Middle and Far West, during the Period of Early American Settlement.* Cleveland: Arthur H. Clark, 1907.
This is the classic collection of first-person accounts of exploring the American West. Included are explorers and travelers along the Canadian River routes to Santa Fe and California.

———, ed. *Original Journals of the Lewis and Clark Expedition.* 8 vols. New York, Dodd, Mead and Company, 1904–1905.
Lewis and Clark obtained some information on the nomadic tribes of the Great Plains.

Underhill, Lonnie E., and Daniel F. Littlefield, Jr. "Wild Turkeys in Oklahoma." *The Chronicles of Oklahoma* 48 (Winter, 1970):376–388.
Describes hunting practices throughout Oklahoma, including the Cheyenne and Arapaho country, during the late 1800s.

Van Zandt, Howard F. "The Battle of the Washita Revisited: Journey to a Historic Site in 1933." *The Chronicles of Oklahoma* 62 (Spring, 1984):56–69.
Van Zandt traveled to the site of the Battle of the Washita and interviewed surviving participants.

Vehik, Susan C. "Cultural Continuity and Discontinuity in the Southern Prairies and Cross Timbers." In *Plains Indians, A.D. 500–1500: The Archaeological Past of Historic Groups*, ed. Karl H. Schiesier. Norman: University of Oklahoma Press, 1994.
Overview of archaeological research on the Southern Plains.

Vestal, Paul A., and Richard E. Schultes. *The Economic Botany of the Kiowa Indians, as it Relates to the History of the Tribe.* Cambridge, Mass.: Botanical Museum of Harvard University, 1939.
Excellent study of plants and their use by the Kiowas.

Wallace, Ernest, and E. Adamson Hoebel. *The Comanches: Lords of the South Plains.* Norman: University of Oklahoma Press, 1952.
Wallace did archival work and interviewed Comanches in 1946, and Hoebel did fieldwork in 1933. The book covers Comanche economy, life cycle, religion, politics, dispute settlement, and warfare. There is a chapter on reservation life up to the allotment process.

Warde, Mary Jane. "Alternative Perspectives on the Battle of Wolf Creek of 1838." *Indigenous Nations Studies Journal* 2 (Fall, 2001):3–14.
This article examines the final confrontation between the Cheyenne-Arapaho alliance and the Kiowa-Comanche-Apache alliance.

———. *Draft Report, Ethnographic Overview and Assessment of the Relationship between Washita Battlefield National Historic Site and the Traditional Associations of the Local Non-Indian Communities and Landowners (Phase IV).* Cooperative Agreement No. 1443CA125098002 (Modification 6). National Park Service, April 2, 2003.
A study of non-Indian occupation of the Cheyenne and Arapaho Reservation.

———. *Final Report, Conduct Oral History Research for Washita Historical Site.* Cooperative Agreement No. 1443CA125098002 (Modification 1). National Park Service, September 30, 1999.
A study of Cheyenne oral history related to the Washita Massacre.

Webb, Walter Prescott. *The Texas Rangers: A Century of Frontier Defense.* Boston: Houghton Mifflin Company, 1935.
The classic work on the history of the Texas Rangers, useful for the Battle of Antelope Hills (Little Robe Creek) in 1858.

Wedel, Mildred Mott. *The Deer Creek Site, Oklahoma: A Wichita Village Sometimes Called Ferdinandina: An Ethnohistorian's View.* Oklahoma City: Oklahoma Historical Society, 1981.
Detailed discussion of how Spanish and French documents help to interpret the Deer Creek site.

———. *The Wichita Indians, 1541–1750: Ethnohistorical Essays.* Lincoln: J and L Reprint Company, 1981.
Excellent discussion of information about Wichitas in Spanish and French sources.

Wedel, Waldo R. *Prehistoric Man on the Great Plains.* Norman: University of Oklahoma Press, 1961.
An overview of the archaeology of the Great Plains that is somewhat dated.

West, James. "Josiah Gregg, 1839–1840." In *Frontier Adventurers: American Exploration in Oklahoma,* ed. Joseph A. Stout. Oklahoma City: Oklahoma Historical Society, 1976.
A description of Gregg's trading venture to Santa Fe by way of the Washita-Canadian divide.

White, Eugene E. *Experiences of a Special Indian Agent.* Norman: University of Oklahoma Press, 1893, 1965 reprint.
White was the federal agent for the Kiowas, Comanches, Apaches, Wichitas, Caddos, and Delawares from 1887 to 1888.

Willibrand, W. A. "In Bilingual Old Okarche." *The Chronicles of Oklahoma* 29 (Fall, 1951):337–354.
Describes German and Anglo-American settlement of Okarche, Oklahoma, along with black/white and Indian/white relations.

Wood, W. Raymond. *Biesterfeldt: A Post-Contact Coalescent Site on the Northeastern Plains. Smithsonian Contributions to Anthropology,* no. 15. Washington, D.C.: General Printing Office, 1971.

A description of excavations of a village located on the Sheyenne River and believed to be Cheyenne.

Wunder, John R. *The Kiowa*. New York: Chelsea House, 1989.
Written for the general audience, the book covers pre-contact times to the 1980s.

100–Year History of Cheyenne and Roger Mills County, Oklahoma. Cheyenne, Okla.: Historic Roger Mills Preservation and Development Foundation, 1992.
A brief pictorial history.

Government Documents

Abert, J. W. "Report." *Message from the President of the United States*. 29th Cong., 1st sess., S. Doc. 438, 1846?
Correspondence and report of the exploration of 1845, with map and engravings of landscape, specifically the Antelope Hills and the divide between the Washita and Canadian rivers.

Burgess, Dent L., Joe D. Nichols, and Odos G. Henson. *Roger Mills County, Oklahoma*.United States Department of Agriculture. Soil Conservation Service. *Survey Bulletin* 59, August 1963.
Useful brief history of Roger Mills County with regard to erosion and flood control measures.

Commissioner of Indian Affairs. *Annual Reports*. Washington: Government Printing Office, 1845–1907.
Annual reports of affairs at Indian agencies, including the Wichita-Caddo and Kiowa-Comanche-Apache agencies. Includes population data.

Marcy, Randolph B. *Exploration of the Red River of Louisiana in the Year 1852*. 33d Cong., 1st sess., H.R. Ex. Doc, 1854.
An account of Marcy's second expedition through southwest Oklahoma with very fine plates of flora, fauna, and geology. Includes a summary of his explorations with a description of the Ft. Smith-Santa Fe Road on the divide between the Washita and Canadian rivers.

————. *Reports of Explorations and Surveys, to Ascertain the Most Practicable and Economical Route for a Railroad from the Mississippi River to the Pacific Ocean, 1853–4*, vol. 3, 33d Cong, 2d sess., S. Ex. Doc. 78, 1856.
Detailed journal of Marcy's second reconnaissance of the Canadian River Valley, this time to survey a railroad route with maps.

Oklahoma Conservation Commission. *Biennial Report*, vol. 1, January 15, 1937.
Brief description of drought and flood problems in western Oklahoma, particularly with reference to the 1934 flood.

Oklahoma State Planning Board. *Preliminary Report on State Planning*, 193. Oklahoma City: State Capitol, 1936.

Included are useful maps and charts showing territorial change and population.

Population, Part 1, Census Reports, vol. 1. *Twelfth Census of the United States Taken in the Year 1900*. Washington, D.C.: United States Census Office, 1901.
Statistical abstract of census data for western Oklahoma counties.

Population—Oklahoma. Thirteenth Census of the United States Taken in the Year 1910. Washington, D.C.: United States Census Office, 1911.
Statistical abstract of census data for western Oklahoma counties.

Population, vol. 3. *Fourteenth Census of the United States Taken in the Year 1920*. Washington, D. C.: General Printing Office, 1923.
Statistical abstract of census data for western Oklahoma counties.

Population, vol. 2. *Sixteenth Census of the United States: 1940*. Washington, D.C.: Government Printing Office, 1943.
Statistical abstract of census data for western Oklahoma counties.

"Report of Lieutenant Colonel G. A. Custer to Major General P. H. Sheridan, in the field on Washita River, November 28, 1868." 40th Cong., 3d sess., S. Ex. Doc. 18. Oklahoma Historical Society, Oklahoma City, Oklahoma.
The field report written by Custer immediately after the Washita Massacre.

"Statement of L. L. Males, Cheyenne, Okla., Representing the Washita Valley Flood Control Council." 83d Cong., 2d sess., House Committee on Agriculture. Microfiche. 83 H1457–1–E, 2260–2261.
Males's update on continuing development of drought and flood alleviation measures in the Washita River Valley.

"Statement of L. L. Males, President, Upper Washita Soil Conservation District, Representing the Elk City Chamber of Commerce." 86th Cong., 1st Sess., Senate Select Committee on National Water Resources. Microfiche, 86 S1376–1–D, 2400–2402.
Males's statement of the need for continuing development of drought and flood alleviation measures in the Washita River Valley.

U.S. Bureau of the Census. *Census of Population: 1970*, vol. 1. *Characteristics of the Population, Part 38, Oklahoma*. Washington, D.C.: General Printing Office, 1973.
Population figures for counties in the former Cheyenne and Arapaho Reservation.

U.S. Bureau of the Census. *Census of Population: 1980*, vol. 1. *Characteristics of the Population, Part 38, Oklahoma*. Washington, D.C.: General Printing Office, 1982.
Population figures for counties in the former Cheyenne and Arapaho Reservation.

U.S. Bureau of the Census. *Census of Population: 1990. Social and Economic Characteristics, Oklahoma*. Washington, D.C.: General Printing Office, 1993.
> Population figures for counties in the former Cheyenne and Arapaho Reservation.

U. S. Senate Reports. 75th Cong., 1st sess., no. 1048, 1937.
> This report includes information concerning Washita River flooding and the need for soil conservation measures.

U.S. War Department. *Senate Reports of Explorations and Surveys to Ascertain the Most Practicable and Economical Route for a Railroad from the Mississippi River to the Pacific Ocean . . . 1853–4*, vol. 3. 33d Cong., 2d sess., S. Ex. Doc. 78, 1856.
> The "Report on the Topographical Features and Character of the Country" for the "Route Near the Thirty-fifth Parallel" contains the account of Lieutenant Amiel Weeks Whipple of his surveying expedition from Fort Smith, Arkansas, by way of the Canadian River toward Tucumcari, New Mexico. Included are drawings and scientific observations of minerals, climate, geology, topography, and other natural features.

Internet Sites

"Black Kettle and McClellan Creek." http://www.fs.fed.us/r2/nebraska/gpng/blmc.html. Retrieved June 4, 2003.
> Description of soil conservation projects that resulted in the creation of Black Kettle National Grassland.

Handbook of Texas Online. http://www.tsha.utexas.edu/handbook/online. February 6, 2002.
> This online encyclopedia, a joint project of the University of Texas and the Texas State Historical Association, provides articles on the Texas Panhandle with suggested bibliography for each topic.

U. S. Bureau of the Census. Population of Counties by Decennial Census, 1900–1990. Oklahoma. http://www.census.gov/population/cencounts/ok199090.txt. Retrieved February 21, 2003.

Manuscript Collections

Oklahoma Historical Society

Camp, Walter, Collection.
> Interview of Ben Clarke [Clark], originally in the Walter Camp Collection, University of Indiana. Section X.

Cheyenne and Arapaho Agency Records.
> Records of the federal agency responsible for the Cheyenne and Arapaho Indians. They include materials on trade, farmers, ranching, transportation, missionaries, and non-Indian residents of the reservation area.

Flemming Loan Register. 1903–1914.
>This register kept by Tom Flemming provides information on land records and economics in Roger Mills County during the second decade of non-Indian settlement.

Indian-Pioneer History. 1937–1938.
>These 112 volumes contain interviews of Indians and pioneers collected by the Works Progress Administration in the late 1930s. Interviewees describe geography, cattle ranching, homesteading, town building, transportation, education, folkways, and many other topics. Indexed by topic and name.

Laird, Mignon, Collection.
>An unprocessed collection including the correspondence and memorabilia of a Cheyenne, Oklahoma, entertainer.

Males, Lorena, Collection.
>An unprocessed collection, which includes Males's newspaper columns about Hammon and Cheyenne, Oklahoma.

Ray, Dee Ann, Collection.
>Included in this unprocessed collection are documents gathered and interviews completed by a librarian and local historian from western Oklahoma.

Whipple, Amiel Weeks, Collection.
>The collection includes journals and maps of Weeks's 1853 expedition, as well as sketches and lithographs by Heinrich Balduin Möllhausen, the German artist who accompanied the expedition.

Western History Collections, University of Oklahoma
Camp Supply Collection.
>A letter book kept by the commissary supply officer during the period 1869–1878, with information about the military occupation of the Cheyenne and Arapaho Reservation and northwestern Oklahoma.

Clark, Ben, Papers. 1863–1907
>Military orders and personal correspondence of an interpreter for the army at Fort Reno, Indian Territory.

Covington, J. A., Diaries. 1863–1900
>Diaries kept by a government employee at the Cheyenne and Arapaho Agency.

Duke, Doris, Collection. 1972. American Indian Oral History.
>Interviews of elderly members of the tribes of Oklahoma. There are seven Wichita interviews (vols. 53–54), thirty-six Kiowa interviews (vols. 33–39), seventeen Apache interviews (vols. 39–42), thirteen Comanche interviews (vols. 27–28), five Caddo interviews (vols. 9–10), two Chickasaw interviews (vol. 26), and fourteen Choctaw interviews (vol. 26).

Ellison, Mrs. C. D., Papers. 1891–1945.
  Included is a pamphlet, *Darlington, the Indian's Friend*, on the life of Cheyenne and Arapaho Agent Brinton Darlington.

Hume, C. Ross, Collection. 1836–1948.
  Hume was the attorney for the Wichita and Affiliated Tribes when they pursued a claim against the federal government. His papers include transcripts of council meetings and interviews with tribal leaders.

Indian-Pioneer Papers. 1937–1938.
  Interviews with Oklahoma residents, including a small number of Indians from western Oklahoma. This collection duplicates the Indian-Pioneer History at the Oklahoma Historical Society but is organized differently.

Marriott, Alice, Papers. 1911–1957.
  The collection contains Marriott's field notes on the Kiowas. She used the notes for her publications. They contain information on the reconstruction of nineteenth-century life.

Murrow, Joseph S., Collection. 1895–1928.
  Microfilmed correspondence, diaries, and reports relating to Baptist missions in Indian Territory. It includes Cheyenne Baptist missions.

Ogden, Florence, Manuscript. 1868–1961.
  The memoir of a resident of Thomas, Oklahoma, describes her childhood and experiences with Cheyenne Indians.

Schmitt, Karl, and Iva O. Schmitt Field Notes. 1947–1950.
  Field notes on various aspects of Wichita life, largely from interviews.

Smith, Paul B. 1832–1883
  Microfilmed reminiscences of Joseph S. Murrow regarding his work with southwestern Oklahoma tribes.

Other Repositories

Hudson's Bay Company Archives. Provincial Archives of Manitoba, Winnipeg, Canada.
  Papers of fur traders who had regular contacts with Gros Ventres in the Saskatchewan area.

Record Group 75. Records of the Bureau of Indian Affairs, National Archives Regional Center, Fort Worth, Texas.
  Reports, files on individuals, and other materials from the Cheyenne-Arapaho Agency.

Scott, Hugh L, Ledger Books. 1889–1897. Fort Sill Museum Archives, Fort Sill, Oklahoma.
  An army officer, Scott interviewed Arapahos and individuals of other tribes about nineteenth-century life.

Maps

Oklahoma Historical Society

Historic Fire Insurance Maps

    Cheyenne, Oklahoma. 1905, 1930

    Hammon, Oklahoma. 1907, 1911, 1913, 1930

    Leedey, Oklahoma. 1930

    Strong City, Oklahoma. 1912, 1930

    Elk City, Oklahoma. 1901, 1902, 1904, 1907, 1910, 1913, 1916, 1922

    Fire insurance maps were drawn periodically to establish insurance rates. Maps detail fire protection facilities, fire hazards, town layout, building materials, building use, and building age, thus providing a snapshot of a town at a specific time.

"Indian Territory, 1889." Rand McNally. Map 2000.208

    Indian Territory, including adjacent areas of the Texas Panhandle. Shows the site of the Battle of the Washita and route of Abert and Peck and of Fort Smith and Albuquerque Road crossing Roger Mills County.

"Map of the Indian Territory, 1866–1890."

    This map of present Oklahoma shows the site of the Battle of the Washita. Places include Seger Colony and Red Moon. Routes include Mobeetie Road and Dodge City Cattle Trail (Great Western Cattle Trail).

"Map Showing Early Trails, Roads, Battle Grounds, and Ranches in the Northwest Part of the Cheyenne and Arrahapho [*sic*] Reservation, 1629–1885."

    Map drawn to accompany Melvin Harrel. "The History of Bar X Lands." *The Chronicles of Oklahoma* 29 (Spring 1951):70–78. Gives an overview of cattle ranching in Roger Mills County and vicinity from 1876 through 1885. Includes a sketch map and very brief descriptions of earlier exploration.

"Oklahoma Railroads." Chicago: Rand, McNally and Company, 1907.

    This map, drawn at statehood, shows the current county boundaries and dense distribution of towns.

"Oklahoma Territory 1898." Frank J. Wikoff Papers.

    Shows Roger Mills and Day counties.

Standard Atlas of Woods County, Oklahoma. Chicago: George A. Ogle and Company, 1906.

    Oklahoma Territorial maps show Day, Roger Mills, and Greer counties before boundaries were redrawn.

1982 Map of Oklahoma's Highway System. Oklahoma Department of Transportation Planning Division, Oklahoma City, Oklahoma.

    This map shows the Sandstone Creek Upstream Flood Control Project area.

"2001–2002 Official State Map." Oklahoma Department of Transportation, Oklahoma City, Oklahoma.
This map shows present-day western Oklahoma.

Oklahoma State University
"New Agricultural and Highway Map of Oklahoma, 1929." State Board of Agriculture, Oklahoma City, Oklahoma. Map Room, Edmond Low Library, Oklahoma State University, Stillwater, Oklahoma.
Shown is Route 66 under construction and one highway through Roger Mills County.

Washita Battlefield National Historic Site
Battlefield on November 27, 1868. *Washita Battlefield National Historic Site Bulletin*, Washita Battlefield National Historic Site, Cheyenne, Oklahoma.

Oklahoma Newspapers

Oklahoma Historical Society (microfilm)
Roger Mills County newspapers and approximate dates
Old Day County papers.   1893–1907
Day County Tribune.   1893
Day County Progress.   1902–1908
Canadian Valley Echo.   *1904–1907*
Hamburg Blade.   1906–1907
Crawford Blade.   1908–1909
Cheyenne Sunbeam.   1894–1906
Berlin Herald.   1906
Cheyenne Roger Mills Sentinel.   1906–1917
Reydon Review.   1932
Cheyenne News.   1938
Strong City Herald.   1912–1918
Strong City Roger Mills Sentinel.   1918
The Western Star (Cheyenne).   1904
Cheyenne Star.   1904–1995
Strong City Herald.   1918–1925
Strong City Press.   1934–1938
Durham Dispatch, 1907
Hammon News.   1910–1912
Hammon Booster.   1913
Hammon Advocate.   1911–1968
Sweetwater Breeze.   1909–1911
Texola Herald.   1904–1910
Texmo Times.   1904–1911
Grand Day County Tribune.   1893–1898
Cheyenne Review.   1986–1989
Also newspapers for other counties in the former Cheyenne and Arapaho Reservation, including *Cheyenne Transporter.*   1880-1886

Oral History

Washita Project Interviews, all in Oklahoma

Phase I: by Mary Jane Warde and Rodger Harris

> Beard, Frances (Cheyenne). El Reno, July 15, 1999
>
> Blackbear, Eugene, Sr. (Cheyenne). Concho, April 21, 1999
>
> Blackbear, Stella "Bessie" Roman Nose (Cheyenne). Watonga, August 25, 1999
>
> Bull Coming, Kathryn (Cheyenne). Seiling vicinity, March 26, 1999
>
> Bull Coming, Vernon (Cheyenne). Seiling vicinity, April 9, 1999
>
> Cometsevah, Colleen (Cheyenne). Clinton, August 20, 1999
>
> Cometsevah, Colleen (Cheyenne). Telephone, September 10, 1999
>
> Cometsevah, Colleen (Cheyenne). Telephone, September 21, 1999
>
> Fletcher, Willie (Cheyenne). Geary, February 2, 1999
>
> Hart, Lawrence (Cheyenne). Oklahoma City, January 14, 1999
>
> Hart, Sam C. (Cheyenne). El Reno, May 19, 1999
>
> Heap of Birds, Alfrich (Cheyenne). Clinton, June 9, 1999
>
> Heap of Birds, Alfrich (Cheyenne). Thomas vicinity, July 23, 1999
>
> Keahbone, Ernie (Kiowa). Anadarko, December 10, 1998
>
> Lonebear, Mary Belle Curtis (Cheyenne). Clinton, July 30, 1999
>
> Osage, Joe (Cheyenne). Hammon, September 1, 1999
>
> Perez, Martha Koomsa (Kiowa). Carnegie, July 14, 1999
>
> Roman Nose, Larry (Cheyenne). El Reno, May 12, 1999
>
> Sage, William (Cheyenne). Anadarko, August 12, 1999
>
> Saupitty, Carney, Sr. (Comanche). Lawton, March 12, 1999
>
> Starr, Moses, Jr. (Cheyenne). Clinton, August 12, 1999
>
> Turtle, Grover (Cheyenne). Watonga, August 25,1999
>
> Twins, Lucian (Cheyenne). Watonga, September 2, 1999
>
> Whitebird, Melvin (Cheyenne). Oklahoma City, August 11, 1999
>
> White Skunk, Carol (Cheyenne). Weatherford, June 7, 1999
>
> Wilson, Terry (Cheyenne). Oklahoma City, February 18, 1999
>
> Youngbull, Lucille (Cheyenne). Clinton, July 29, 1999

Phase II: by Loretta Fowler, Jim Anquoe, and Moses Starr

> Big Medicine, Joe (Cheyenne). Watonga, August 19, 2000
>
> Blackbear, Eugene, Sr. (Cheyenne). Moore, September 20, 2000
>
> Cometsevah, Laird (Cheyenne). Clinton, March 9, 2001
>
> Cometsevah, Laird (Cheyenne). Clinton, March 30, 2001
>
> Fletcher, John, Sr.* (Arapaho). Geary, March 2, 2001
>
> Haag, Rollin (Cheyenne). Calumet, December 18, 2000
>
> Hoffman, Archie (Cheyenne). Concho, September 15, 2000
>
> Pewo, Edwin (Cheyenne). Hammon, April 4, 2001
>
> Starr, Moses, Sr. (Cheyenne). Weatherford, March 26, 2001
>
> Starr, Moses, Sr. (Cheyenne). Weatherford, March 28, 2001
>
> Starr, Moses, Sr. (Cheyenne). Weatherford, April 13, 2001
>
> White Shield, Blanche (Cheyenne). Hammon, April 16, 2001
>
> Wilson, Bertha (Cheyenne). Weatherford, April 13, 2001

Phase III: by Loretta Fowler and Jim Anquoe
    Anquoe, Jack (Kiowa). Tulsa, January 10, 2003
    Carter, Cecile Elkins (Caddo). Meade, December 13, 2002
    Chalepah, Alonzo (Apache). Anadarko, March 21, 2003
    Daugomah, Lu Creda Weller (Caddo). Gracemont, December 16, 2002
    Horse, Ella Faye (Kiowa). Carnegie, December 4, 2002
    Koomsa, Martha (Perez) (Kiowa). Carnegie, November 25, 2002
    McAdams, Gary (Wichita). Anadarko, November 8, 2002
    McDaniel, Eleanor (Comanche). Cache, September 18, 2002
    Niedo, Ray (Comanche). Cache, October 4, 2002
    Owings, Stuart (Wichita). Anadarko, November 8, 2002
    Tahbone, George (Kiowa). Mountain View, December 11, 2002

Phase IV: by Mary Jane Warde, Rodger Harris, and Dennis Zotigh
    Amen, Delbert (Non-Indian). Oklahoma City, October 15, 2002
    Chalfant, Billy (Non-Indian). Cheyenne, July 9, 2002
    Crane, Glena Belle Savage (Non-Indian). Cheyenne, February 19, 2002
    Davis, Clara R. King, and Lester R. Davis (Non-Indians). Cheyenne vicinity, October 16, 2002
    Duke, Bob (Non-Indian). Oklahoma City, January 8, 2003
    Heisch, Melvena Thurman (Non-Indian). Oklahoma City, July 5, 2002
    Hensley, Manuel C. (Non-Indian). Strong City, October 16, 2002
    Males, Lorena Savage (Non-Indian). Cheyenne, February 20, 2002
    Peters, David (Non-Indian). Stillwater, September 14, 2002
    Tracy, Dale, Collier Tracy, and Judy Tracy (Non-Indians). Cheyenne vicinity, July 9, 2002
    Tracy, Judy (Non-Indian). Cheyenne vicinity, July 9, 2002

*Both Cheyenne and Arapaho, John Fletcher chose to identify himself as an Arapaho.

Indian-Pioneer History, Oklahoma Historical Society
Interviews of Cheyenne and Arapaho Reservation settlers, 1892 through 1938, by volume and page numbers
    Allen, H. L.   77:15–16
    Austin, Bertie.   72:96–98
    Bradley, LeRoy.   77:260–267
    Coleman, Frank Andrew.   100:118–124
    Creason, Owen Henry.   100:366–374
    Curl, W. S.   65:384–388
    Dane, Alfred W.   65:397–399
    Ellis, Albert H.   74:89
    Ewing, Frank.   79:295–504
    Gillbreath, J. C.   84:163–168
    Gillian, Robert H.   80:134–137
    Gray, E. C. et al.   84:296–397

Green, Anna L.   84:361–371
Griffin, Anna.   80:199–202
Hancock, Georgia.   92:168–174
Harrell, J. C.   92:220–221
Hatchett, Joel F.   92:305
Henderson, Willie Theo Ormand.   80:414–423
Hendrix, Adlai M.   74:338–339
Henry, B. B.   92:394–396
Hickman, Mrs. W. P.   92:457–460
Innis, Joseph A.   30:430–438
Johnson, Nettie Rosser.   31:282–284
Martain, Mrs. S. J.   108:86–92
McKay, William.   35:269
McMillian, Samuel L.   71:210
McReynolds, Mary.   35:433–440
McRill, Albert L.   76:156
Miller, John G.   36:302–304
Mitchell, Dick.   60:378–381
Moffet, Dave.   108:342–343
Moore, Rosa Ward Hornberger.   81:95–100
Morgan, Julie Ann.   81:103–107
Morgan, Lydia.   107:108–113
Northrip, M. A.   107:242–252
Null, Omar E.   76:258–260; 102:472–511
Ponder, W. P.   40:203–205
Pyle, B. F.   93:518–526
Ragains, Jannie.   41:119–120
Ranck, Linnaeus B.   113:145–189
Ravenscraft, Lot.   76:392–393
Ray, T. J.   113:256
Richards, O. H.   76:408; 82:36–38
Ross, Adah I.   42:327–342
Sackett, Eliza J.   101:3–4
Shanley, Mrs. U. T.   101:106–217
Simpson, J. D.   58:245
Skelton, T. F.   101:436–438
Slatten, H. W.   101:469–472
Staton, Mrs. W. E.   68:106–107
Stewart, William B.   68:137–149
Stubbs, James Allen.   87:434–444
Sutton, F. D.   87:489–495
Timmons, Annie I.   112:245–248
Treadaway, Henry C.   112:393–394; 112:397–400
Turner, Nat.   58:426
Walck, H. I.   75:20–26
Wall, Mary Rutherford.   48:340–343
Williams, John.   94:189
Wright, W. E.   50:497–504

Oral History Collection, Oklahoma Historical Society
Interviews on the Great Depression, Northwest Oklahoma

Adams, Grace. 84.137
Adams, Russell. V85.064
Alexander, Nellie 84.100.A–B
Alley, C. L. V85.135
Baird, Ralph, Jr. V85.009
Baird, Ralph, Sr. V85.030
Barth, Victor. V85.072
Beck, Helen. V84.128
Blackmon, Ezra. V84.140
Bodenhamer, Hal. LL203
Bouse, Leo. 85.031
Cammerer, Albert. V84.119
Carpenter, Robert. V88.100
Chappel, Ralph H. V85.118
Chrispin, Carroll Clyde. V86.060
Clark, Edna. 84.144
Cook, A. R. LL501
Cotter, Lee. 83.112
Crigler, Wesley. 85.028
Cronkite, Lillian. 84.082
Crooks, Goldie and Carl Long. 85.138.A–B
Cully, Ernest. 84.164
Day, Bertha M. V86.074
Davison, Francis. 85.037.A–B
Dixon, Mrs. Floyd. 84.094
Ediger, Metta. V84.135
Elmore, George. 85.034
Elmore, Stella. V87.284
Eoff, Esther Marcella. V84.118
Epperly, W. G. V85.114
Erlich, Bill. 86.016
Erlich, Willie. V86.037
Farr, Doane. LL203
Flaherty, Lois Fryer. 85.082.A–B
Frost, Francis Brandon.V87.178
Frye, Mr. and Mrs. Garnett. 86.007.A–C
Ganes, Clay. 84.181.A–B
Gibbens, Agnes M. V85.079
Gillenwater, Harold. V87.185
Gorem, Woodrow. 84.075
Hayes, Jennie. V85.054
Hays, Lillian. 83.041
Hepner, Arthur. V87.078
Hinton, Ruth, Carrie Leslie, and Bess Calk. 82.011
Hoch, Roy, and Bessie O'Hair. 84.153.A–B
Holt, Willard D. 83.143
Howard, Robert. 84.139

Howe, Mary Strange.   84.072.A–B
Hudson, Fred.   84.098
Hunt, Mildred Blair.   V86.076
Jackson, Brice.   84.099
Jackson, Willia Mae.   V85.060
Johnson, Luella.   85.115
Jordan, Ethel.   84.078
Judy, B. G. Hubert.   V84.136
K–101 Radio "Black Sunday."   84.112.C
Kamas, Lewis.   87.002
Kamas, Mary.   LL594.2
Kellerman, Frederick.   V85.071
Kelly, Clemon.   84.081
Kennedy, Sue.   85.131
King, Ethel.   84.154.A–B
King, Venus B.   LL477
Klein, Helen.   V86.026
Lackey, Toney.   83.107.A–B
LaMunyon, Cassius.   87.018
Larason, Albert R.   V85.140
Litz, Walter, and Mary Norton.   84.155.A–B
Logan, Martha.   85.012
Long, Carl, and Goldie Crooks.   85.138.A–B
Long, Maude Marie.   85.164
Luinstra, Tiny.   85.008
Mades, Pearl.   83.022
Marston, John D.   V87.271
McFarland, John.   84.076.A–B
McHard, Mildred.   83.010
McQuigg, Okla Dearing, and Melba Dearing Bullar.   85.042
Merrill, Lloyd.   84.109
Mickley, Mable.   83.111.A–B
Miller, Mildred.   84.167
Minton, Theophilus "Jack."   85.175.A–B
Mix, Maude.   V84.147.A–B
Moore, Lowell.   84.170.A–B
Morris, John.   LL800
Mote, Lile.   V85.067
Munson, Thomas.   87.051
Oates, Vernie.   V84.172
O'Hair, Noah.   V84.146
Packard, Myrtle.   83.099
Patterson, Marcella.   V88.023
Pauls, George.   V84.169
Phillips, Kenneth.   V85.014
Phillips, Raymond.   87.167.A–B
Prophet, Cora.   84.163.A–B
Quisenberry, Turner.   V87.180
Rader, Bonnie.   84.180.A–B

Elk City (Oklahoma) Carnegie Library: Living Legends Project

Alee, Bob.   1977.   2 tapes

Bowers, Bernice, and Humphrey and Ruth McNatt. Foss, Oklahoma. 1975

Campbell, Rex.   1976

Coates, Mrs. Olice.   1977

Gregory, Dona (Mrs. H. M.).   2 tapes

Hill, Iris.   1976.   2 tapes

Hunter, Vern.   1977

Joseph, Vern.   1977

Lindley, Ernel Mae.   1975

Massey, Viola.   1977.   2 tapes

Morrow, Sterling.   1977

Ramsey, Etta Musick.   2 tapes

Royse, Barbara Elizabeth.   1976

Smith, W. G.   1976.   2 tapes

Story, Ed.   1976.   7 tapes

Sullins, Mrs. J. W.   1975

Whited, Belle. Whited Grist Mill.   1979

Visit of President Jimmy Carter, 1979
   Carter's Town Meeting
   Carter's Visit to First Baptist Church
   First Baptist Church Services
   Planning Meeting
   Story, Ed.   1988

ABOUT THE AUTHOR

Mary Jane Warde earned her doctorate in Western and American history from Oklahoma State University in 1991. Winner of the Muriel Wright Award for the outstanding article in *The Chronicles of Oklahoma* in 1993, she has authored several articles and a biography, *George Washington Grayson and the Creek Nation, 1843–1920*. She has been Indian Historian at the Oklahoma Historical Society since 1998.